# POMPEII A·D 79

## Volume I

Treasures from the
National Archaeological Museum,
Naples, and the
Pompeii Antiquarium

Made possible by grants from
The National Endowment
for the Humanities and
Xerox Corporation

Museum of Fine Arts, Boston
The Art Institute of Chicago
Dallas Museum of Fine Arts
American Museum of Natural History
1978-1979

# POMPEII A·D 79

Copyright © 1978
by Museum of Fine Arts
Boston, Massachusetts

Library of Congress catalogue card no. 78-54015

ISBN 0-87846-124-8

Typeset by Wrightson Typographers
Newton, Massachusetts

Printed in U.S.A.
by Case-Hoyt, Rochester, New York

Designed by Carl Zahn

Cover:
**61**
**Mosaic portrait of a woman**
Height 25.5 cm, width 20.5 cm
From a small *cubiculum* in House VI, 15, 14

Portrait, probably from life, of a young woman.
Her hair is parted centrally and tied behind with
a ribbon. She wears earrings of pearls set in gold,
a pearl necklace with a gold clasp set with precious stones, and a dark, low-necked dress, which
shows through a gold-embroidered transparent
veil. Dress and jewelry suggest a woman of rank.

This is a studio piece *(emblema)* made with
very small tesserae, shaped and toned, set within
a shallow, tray-like limestone frame. It was
found in the center of an *opus sectile* pavement
made up of hexagons, lozenges, and triangles of
blue-gray, white, and red marble, dating from
the last period before A.D. 79. In this context it
was almost certainly reused. The mosaic itself
can hardly be later than the end of the first
century B.C.

Title page:
**1**
**Pair of villa landscapes**
Width 53 cm, height 22 cm
From Pompeii

Two separate views of villa façades probably
from the lateral panels of a Third Style scheme
(see illustration, p. 27), now mounted as a pair.
The left-hand view shows a straight porticoed
façade upraised on a platform with a tall columnar central porch; in front of the portico is a garden with a large axial enclosure and at either end,
rising from a lower level, is a double portico, of
two orders, facing outward. Above and beyond
the right-hand portico is the façade of a temple-
like building facing inward; there may have been
other buildings or trees in the damaged upper
left-hand part. The right-hand view shows a central gabled porch at the junction of two gable-
ended, inward-facing porticoes, enclosing on
three sides a trapezoidal space concentric to
which is an enclosure with posts at the angles.
Above and behind rise a number of other buildings including a circular *tempietto (tholos)* and
another colonnade. The perspective of these
scenes is syntactic, and some of the detail (e.g.,
the half-gables of the flanking porticoes on the
left-hand panel) is without parallel in surviving
contemporary architecture, but it is generally
accepted that such façades were a feature of the
wealthy *villae marittimae*.

*All objects shown in color plates*
*are from the National Archaeological Museum,*
*Naples*

# PREFACE

The catastrophic events of August 24, A.D. 79, that submerged Herculaneum and Pompeii in an avalanche of ashes, pumice, and volcanic mud brought life in these prosperous Roman towns to a sudden and total stop. Through the ages the volcanic debris that so tragically cut short the life of the inhabitants acted as a protective layer shielding the towns with all that was inside from the ravages of time. Unearthed by archaeologists in the course of excavations that extend over more than two centuries, the objects are preserved very much as they were 1,900 years ago.

As we walk along the streets and enter the villas of the rich and the taverns of the poor, it is as if the occupants had gone a moment ago to one of the many shops, to the theater, or to one of the temples in which they paid homage to their many different gods. The colorful story of their life unfolds before our eyes as we see the paintings that adorned the walls of their houses, the inexhaustible variety of paraphernalia that surrounded them, the utensils they used, and the games they played until the moment of the catastrophe. The exhibition "Pompeii A.D. 79" consists of many rare and beautiful works of art that can be viewed and admired for their own intrinsic artistic merit. But above and beyond that the exhibited pieces together evoke the spirit of the people of Pompeii and make us understand how they lived, what their aspirations were, and what they believed in.

Now that "Pompeii A.D. 79," after its unprecedented success in the capitals of Europe, begins its triumphal tour of the United States, I consider it a privilege to acknowledge our deep indebtedness to all of those who have made this unique cultural manifestation possible.

First and foremost we wish to express our deep gratitude to the government of the Republic of Italy, the Ministry of Foreign Affairs, and the Ministry of Cultural Heritage for their gracious permission to have this exhibition of great cultural treasures travel to the United States. We especially thank His Excellency Dr. Vittorio Cordero de Montezemolo, formerly Director General for Cultural, Scientific, and Technological Cooperation, Ministry of Foreign Affairs; his successor in that office, His Excellency Sergio Romano; and His Excellency Raniero Paolucci di Calboli, Vice-Director, Directorate General for Cultural, Scientific,

and Technological Cooperation, Ministry of Foreign Affairs, for their help and advice during the negotiations; we also thank Dr. Guglielmo Triches, Director General for Antiquities and Fine Arts, Ministry of Cultural Heritage, for his generous help in the decisions on sites and schedules.

Many demanding tasks connected with preparing the exhibition were patiently and efficiently discharged by the staffs of the Naples Museum and the Pompeii Antiquarium, and we gratefully acknowledge the cooperation of Professor Fausto Zevi, Superintendent of Antiquities, Naples and Caserta; Dr. Enrica Pozzi-Paolini, Director of the National Archaeological Museum, Naples; and Dr. Maria Giuseppina Cerulli-Irelli, Director of Excavations, Pompeii. Dr. Marco Miele, Director of the Italian Cultural Institute, New York, acted as an invaluable intermediary with the Italian authorities. His constant interest and encouragement has been highly appreciated. We also wish to express our thanks to Alitalia for the special care with which they handled the shipments from Naples to Boston.

On the United States side we would like to thank first of all The Honorable John Volpe, formerly United States Ambassador to Italy, whose enthusiastic response when first approached with our proposal created the first impetus toward the realization of this project. His successor, The Honorable Richard N. Gardner, assisted by Richard T. Arndt, Cultural Affairs Officer, and Mrs. Susan Lowe Modi, Assistant Cultural Attaché, provided the indispensable liaison with the Italian authorities. They were most helpful and generous with their experienced advice.

The exhibition is made possible by grants from the National Endowment for the Humanities and Xerox Corporation; it is supported by a Federal Indemnity from the Federal Council on the Arts and Humanities. The liaison with our corporate sponsor was provided by Ruder & Finn.

A project of this scope and importance involves many people and leaves hardly any department of a museum unaffected. It was logical, however, that the primary responsibility for "Pompeii A.D. 79" should rest with the Department of Classical Art, which has responded with an enthusiasm that permeated the entire organization. John Herrmann, assistant curator of classi-

cal art, was involved in the project from its very inception and followed it through to completion. The other members of the Department of Classical Art, Kristin Anderson, Miriam Braverman, Mary Comstock, Ariel Herrmann, Emily Vermeule, Cornelius Vermeule, and Florence Wolsky, each made their own contribution to the exhibition and its catalogue. Judy Spear edited volume one, Margaret Jupe volume two.

We thank John Ward-Perkins and Amanda Claridge for their permission to use a large part of the text of the English catalogue for the catalogue of the American exhibition. We gratefully acknowledge the cooperation of Imperial Tobacco Ltd. and *The Daily Telegraph,* the sponsors of the exhibition at the Royal Academy in London. We thank Dietrich von Bothmer and the Metropolitan Museum of Art for their permission to install the Boscotrecase frescoes and Polaroid Corporation for the special large-size photographs that complement this part of the exhibition.

To name all of those in the four participating museums who have contributed to this unique cultural manifestation is impossible. May all enjoy the exhibition with a sense of gratitude and pride.

JAN FONTEIN, *Director*
*Museum of Fine Arts, Boston*

**2**
**Painting of a villa beside the sea**
Diameter 25 cm
From Stabiae

Roundel portraying the two-storied columnar
façade of a *villa marittima*. The center of the
façade curves inward, toward a tower-like circular feature. In front is a platform with two projecting jetties, human figures, and statues.

5
**Painting of a sanctuary beside the sea**
Width 62 cm, height 52 cm
From Pompeii

This fragment portrays a sanctuary, set on a rocky island or promontory, and in the foreground two boats. The details of the sanctuary are conventional: a central, circular shrine, or *tholos*, flanked by porticoes and a re-entrant façade wall; in front of this, facing onto the water, is an open platform, on which are several groups of figures, including a woman and a dog.

# FOREWORD

The arts in America are flourishing today as they never have before in the history of our nation. Unprecedented interest in museum exhibitions, theater, dance, and music is evident in record-high attendance not only at traditional institutions in major urban centers but throughout the country wherever artistic activities are taking place. Equally evident is a surge in creative activity by Americans in both the performing and visual arts, thus giving our cultural environment a new and distinctly American flavor.

If we search for meaning in this expansion of interest in the arts, we can recognize the signs of our maturity both as a nation and as a people. After 200 years of youthful impetuosity, we are embarking on the process of introspection and delving into the past in order to understand and appreciate the present. We have begun to realize that a sense of history is a prerequisite for a purposeful existence.

We are at the dawn of a new era for Americans. If we are to make the most of the opportunities presented to us, we must marshal every resource to permit the arts their full expression and to incorporate the arts of the past into our definition of the future. This task is a formidable one, but it will be accomplished if governmental, academic, and business institutions can be encouraged to contribute their support. It is in this spirit that Xerox has undertaken to sponsor in association with the National Endowment for the Humanities this extraordinary exhibition.

It is our hope that when future historians comment on our society, they will note that this was a time when America came of age by rewarding the arts with the support they both deserve and require.

We wish to acknowledge with gratitude the efforts of the Italian Government, which made it possible to bring this exhibition to the United States. We are indeed proud to be associated, through "Pompeii A.D. 79" with four of our country's most prestigious museums: the Museum of Fine Arts in Boston, which organized the exhibition; the Art Institute of Chicago; the Dallas Museum of Fine Arts; and the American Museum of Natural History in New York.

C. PETER MCCOLOUGH
*Chairman and Chief Executive Officer*
*Xerox Corporation*

Few events in ancient history are as widely known as Pompeii and what happened there on a sunny August day 1,900 years ago. And few events in history demonstrate so aptly the fragile quality of man and of his fabrications—or the value of the studies we collectively call the humanities.

But it would be a mistake to think of an exhibition like this splendid "Pompeii A.D. 79" as the whole objective, or the centerpiece of effort for the National Endowment for the Humanities. As imaginative as it is, and as thorough, and as scholarly, it should not overshadow the larger number of domestic exhibitions aided by NEH which draw from American collections to provide insight into foreign cultures or to show the variety of American, local, regional, or ethnic heritage.

The role of the full-scale international exhibition is important. The National Endowment for the Humanities has been pleased to have been able to contribute to a vast variety of educational experiences through interpretive museum exhibitions which have enriched the lives of millions of our citizens. Each of the major international exhibitions of the past four years—the impressionist paintings from the Leningrad Hermitage in 1973, the French tapestry exhibition in 1974, the Chinese archaeological exhibition, the Scythian gold exhibition, and the "Treasures of Tutankhamun" exhibition now traveling to six regions of the U.S.—has received wide and enthusiastic public response. We believe the kind of response and the kind of interest that has followed these past efforts of the Endowment will be repeated with "Pompeii A.D. 79."

But it is not the King Tuts and the Scythian Golds—as strong as they have been as education tools for the public—which form the backbone of the Endowment's support of public humanities programs in museums and historical organizations. While the larger exhibitions are winning headlines and drawing metropolitan crowds, quieter and no less important events are occurring in American county seats and towns. More than 200 grants to historical organizations, art museums, science museums, natural history museums, and children's museums have also been made. And the Endowment's interest is always the same: to broaden the public understanding of the humanistic aspects of our heritage—the political, economic, social, religious, and cultural history and the interaction between these human experiences and the natural world. This is our conception of the role of the museum—as an instrument for explanation of the world which we as humans have inherited.

JOSEPH D. DUFFEY, *Chairman*
*National Endowment for the Humanities*

8

# CONTENTS
## Volume I

PREFACE, *page 5*

FOREWORD, *page 8*

INTRODUCTION, *page 11*

CAMPANIA, *page 13*

HISTORY OF POMPEII, *page 33*

THE TOWN: GOVERNMENT AND PEOPLE, *page 39*

THE TOWN: PLANNING AND ARCHITECTURE, *page 45*

THE POMPEIAN HOUSE AND GARDEN, *page 52*

THE ECONOMY: AGRICULTURE AND INDUSTRY, *page 59*

CULTS AND BELIEFS, *page 63*

ENTERTAINMENT, SPORT, AND LEISURE, *page 87*

PAINTING, *page 97*

SCULPTURE, *page 105*

THE OTHER ARTS, *page 108*

HERCULANEUM, *page 110*

The Forum at Pompeii,
Vesuvius in background

House of Neptune and Amphitrite
at Herculaneum

# INTRODUCTION

*Authors' note*

We could not have written this catalogue had it not been for the unstinted help we have received from many friends, among them Simon Bendall, Joanna Bird, John Callaghan, Maria Giuseppina Cerulli-Irelli, Anna Fazzari, Martin Frederiksen, Antonio Giuliano, Wilhelmina Jashemski, Anne Laidlaw, Demetrios Michaelides, Massimo Pallottino, Toby Parker, Enrica Pozzi Paolini, Dale Trendall, Luciana Valentini, Angela Wardle, Helen Whitehouse, and Fausto Zevi. But there have been many others as well, too numerous to name individually. To all of them we offer our sincere thanks.

We would also like to take this opportunity of expressing our deep sense of personal gratitude to our Italian friends, both in Naples and in Rome, who gave us so much of their time and trouble in resolving the thousand and one difficulties, great and small, that inevitably arise in the preparation of an enterprise of this sort and size. But for their patience, understanding, and unfailing kindness, it would have been a very different story. We are very conscious of our debt.

This is not the first time, and it will surely not be the last, that the authors of an exhibition catalogue have had to do their work far more hurriedly than they would have wished, often without any possibility of reference back to the objects themselves to resolve doubtful points. We have aimed at accuracy, but we are all too aware that we have not always achieved it.

JOHN WARD-PERKINS
AMANDA CLARIDGE

On the morning of the twenty-fourth of August, A.D. 79, the long-dormant volcano of Vesuvius blew up, and by the evening of that day the two flourishing towns of Pompeii and Herculaneum and the nearby coastal resort of Stabiae were dead, already half-buried by the rain of ash, pumice, and volcanic mud beneath which they were to lie entombed for more than sixteen centuries. Before long their very locations were lost. It was not until 1709 that well-diggers hit upon the theater of Herculaneum, and it was another thirty years before, in 1738, the Bourbons put in hand the program of organized treasure hunting (*zufälliges raüberisches Nachwühlen,* "haphazard, predatory grubbing," is how Goethe described it) that furnished the first nucleus of the royal collections that were eventually to come to rest in the National Museum of Naples. Then in 1748 attention was diverted to another Vesuvian site, where peasants had recently made promising finds and where digging was easier. This proved to be the lost Pompeii. Here too exploration was at first haphazard and destructive, and it was really only with the appointment of Giuseppe Fiorelli (1860-1875) that systematic excavation may be said to have started. It was he who hit upon the idea of making casts of the victims of the eruption, and who introduced the system of nomenclature, still in use today, whereby any building in the town can be located in terms of its region, its city block, and the serial numbers of its street entrances. It was again he and his successor, Michele Ruggiero, who first adopted the modern principle of restoring buildings and of conserving finds in place, instead of ripping out the more spectacular and leaving the rest to disintegrate.

The first and overwhelming impression these sites leave on the modern visitor today is the immediacy of this ancient tragedy. As one gazes on the table set for breakfast, on the posters for the next municipal elections, on the pathetic huddle of bodies clustered in a cellar, the intervening centuries fall away. It is just as if yesterday some sudden and dreadful natural catastrophe had overwhelmed all the familiar things of one's hometown, preserving every intimate detail of the houses and the supermarket for the archaeologists of future millennia. This sense of yesterday, this powerfully enduring presence of all the little everyday things that constitute the externals of a way of life, this is something unique to Pompeii and Herculaneum.

But it is not the tragedy of 24 August A.D. 79 as such that is the subject of this exhibition. We are concerned with one particular aspect of the event, namely to present, so far as is possible in terms of objects that can be transported, a cross-section of the art and craftsmanship of the buried cities, as it stood at the moment when the clock of history was so dramatically stopped: that of Pompeii in the first instance, because the setting is there more complete and the range of available material wider, but supplemented where necessary from Herculaneum, from Stabiae, and from material now in the National Museum of Naples of which the precise Vesuvian source is no longer known.

Art and craftsmanship: one uses the double term advisedly because the modern distinction between artist and craftsman would have had very little meaning, at any rate with reference to contemporary artists. Throughout most of classical antiquity, and very much so in Roman times, the artist was by definition a craftsman, working to supply the specific needs of a patron or, more generally, the demands of public taste. This fact is bound to influence any modern attempt to present his work. Certain categories and certain individual products of ancient art may be timeless, transcending all accidents of time and place. It does not really matter that a fifth-century Athenian viewed the Parthenon frieze under very different conditions from ourselves, and with very different eyes: the quality still shines through. Even so, there can be very few products of ancient art that do not gain an added dimension from being viewed within their historical and social context. This is emphatically true when the objects in question are the products of a society as complex and many-sided as that of Rome, and doubly true when they represent not some single, homogeneous masterpiece, nor the accumulated artistic treasure of some single great patron, but a selection of the objects that just happened to be assembled on the walls and in the streets of a town of provincial Italy on that fateful August day when, without warning, history stood still.

One has therefore to present the art of Pompeii in its context. In the case of the paintings this is quite literally true, physically as well as metaphorically. The Romans did possess panel paintings, as we do, but very few of these have survived, and the paintings that now adorn the walls of museums and galleries were all once parts of much larger decorative complexes, detached from which they have much the same artistic significance as a panel cut from a Tiepolo ceiling. We can still enjoy many of their qualities, but viewed in isolation they have certainly lost something of their original artistic intention. One has to remember too that the artists who painted them, most of them simple craftsmen, both slaves and freedmen, were operating within a context of ideas very different from our own. Many of the presuppositions of the society for which Tiepolo and his assistants worked are still common currency, making it relatively easy for us to enter into the spirit of their work. Roman society is a very different matter. It is true that certain aspects of the daily life of Pompeii do strike a startling note of modernity. Water supply and sanitation; paving and street drainage, and the organization of such public services as markets and the disposal of refuse; the mechanisms of commerce and banking; the life of the tavern and bar; the addiction to spectator sport; all of these are still quite near enough to our own recent past (and indeed in some cases to our present) to strike an immediate response of comfortable recognition. But the moment one scratches a little deeper, one is aware also of a number of profound, underlying differences. The position of the family within the social structure, religious beliefs and ethics, the status of the professions, the accepted functions and duties of patronage, these are some only of the aspects of Pompeian life without some awareness of which it is very hard to arrive at any true evaluation of the material remains. The art of Pompeii was an integral part of this wider culture.

An exhibition can and should concentrate on allowing the objects displayed to speak for themselves. We hope that by our selection and our presentation we may have conveyed something also of the wider message that, unbeknown to itself, Roman Pompeii was busy compiling for us to read.

# CAMPANIA

*Sketch map to show the possible position of the port, the mouth, and ancient course of the river Sarno in relation to Pompeii. Country villas in the neighborhood are indicated by an open circle.*

1. *Villa Rustica, Boscoreale*
2. *Villa of P. Fannius Synistor, Boscoreale*
3. *Villa of Agrippa Postumus, Boscotrecase*
4. *Oplontis*
5. *Villa of the Mysteries*
6. *Villa of Diomedes*
7. *Temple of Dionysus, S. Abbondio*
8. *Large storerooms, shops, and other buildings belonging to the port*

Today, a century after the unification of modern Italy, it is not always easy to recall that what was achieved in 1870 was not the restoration of a natural, self-evident state of affairs that had been briefly disrupted by external forces; it was the re-creation of a national entity that had been laboriously built up by classical Rome, only to disintegrate into its component parts as soon as the authority of the Western Roman Empire collapsed. One of the geographical units that make up Italy is Campania, the region of which Naples is today the capital. Long before it was a part of Roman Italy Pompeii had been a city of Campania, and for two of the three thousand-odd years since central Italy first emerges into history Campania has been independent of, and frequently in conflict with, Rome. Somewhere between Rome and Naples the South begins. This is still one of the salient facts of Italian political and economic life and it is a truth rooted in history.

The heart of Campania has always been the Bay of Naples, together with the fertile coastal plain that is bounded on the north by the river Volturno and on the east and south by the western slopes of the Apennines and the mountains of the Sorrento peninsula. Both geographically and historically it constitutes a remarkably well-defined unit. Except for the mountains to the south and east, this is all very fertile country of recent volcanic origin, and it first took historical shape when in the eighth century B.C. the Greeks, finding themselves debarred from further progress up the western coast by the Etruscans, and later by the Romans, established here a number of thriving settlements. During the course of the fifth century B.C. these Greek colonies and trading stations, together with the Etruscan outpost of Capua, lost their independence, passing under the control of Italic tribesmen who had moved down from the mountains of the interior. The latter were quick to learn the lessons of civilization and the union was a fruitful one, resulting in a culture that in varying proportions was both Greek and Italic. Campania never lost its Greek cultural roots or its Greek commercial contacts and aptitudes; but at the same time the Italic component remained strong enough to enable this mixed society to adapt without too much difficulty to the consequences of the inexorable southward advance of Rome. Whereas over much of southern Italy the Roman conquest was a sorry story of pillage, disruption, and catastrophic economic decline, Campania was the exception. Power and authority had moved to Rome, but in terms of commerce, culture, and the arts Campania enjoyed a prosperity fully equal to, and in certain respects in advance of, that of Rome itself.

The history of Pompeii, summarized in the following section, is in most respects that of Campania in miniature, but we may single out two aspects of the broader scene that were especially important for the cultural and artistic life of the Campanian cities. One was the fact that until the emperor Claudius created his new, artificial harbor at the mouth of the Tiber, the chief seagoing port of Rome was Puteoli, the modern Pozzuoli. With the establishment of Rome as a world power in the second century B.C. came, inevitably, great material prosperity, one facet of which was the settlement at Puteoli of a large and prosperous commercial community, derived very largely from the Hellenistic East. It is symptomatic that as early as 105 B.C. Puteoli should already have had a temple of the Egyptian divinities Isis and Serapis, and there are many traces of other oriental cults. Puteoli was where St. Paul landed on his journey to Rome.

Another aspect of the Campanian scene very closely related to Rome's new-found position as a world power was that of the changes that the sudden access of wealth inevitably brought about in Roman upper class customs. Among these

Facing page:
**217**
**Wall painting: sacro-idyllic landscape with shepherd and goats** (detail)
Height 50 cm, width 49 cm
From Pompeii, exact location unknown

Landscape from the center of a wall panel, probably of the Fourth Style. It portrays an idealized rustic shrine, set within a rocky landscape with trees. In the foreground a man is pushing a goat toward the shrine, perhaps for sacrifice.

**153**
**Wall painting: the Three Graces**
Width 53 cm, height 56 cm
From the *tablinum* of the House of Titus Dentatus Panthera (IX, 2, 16)

Panel cut from the middle of a Fourth Style wall. The Three Graces, or *Charites*, daughters of Zeus by various mothers, personified beauty, grace, and intellectual and moral wisdom. There are innumerable examples of this group both in painting and in sculpture, all obviously copied from the same original, presumably a well-known Hellenistic sculpture. The Graces are commonly portrayed, as here, holding or wreathed with spring flowers. This explains the presence of flowers in the landscape setting, a feature not represented elsewhere in Pompeian mythological scenes.

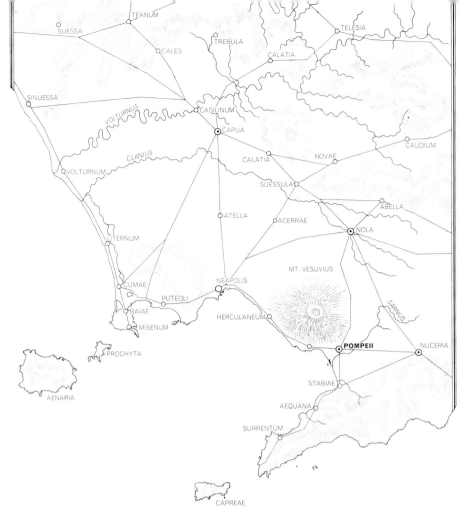

Roman Campania

was one that calls for no comment today, namely the determination of every well-to-do Roman to acquire a seaside property. Gaius Marius had a villa at Misenum, Sulla the Dictator one near Cumae. Among the many prominent Romans known to have possessed such seaside retreats during the last half-century of the Republic were Julius Caesar, Pompey, Lucullus, the notorious Clodia, Varro the historian, many distinguished ex-consuls, and several of Cicero's clients; Cicero himself had no less than three Campanian properties, at Cumae, at Puteoli, and at Pompeii. By the time the emperor Augustus established himself on Capri, the Bay of Naples was ringed around with the playgrounds of the rich. As we shall see, these *villae marittimae* constituted a natural field for imaginative architectural experiment, while at the same time they ensured that the decorative tastes and fashions of Roman society found an almost immediate expression in Campania, and vice versa. They were also a bountiful source of artistic patronage. Each year there is fresh evidence to show that the Bay of Naples, and especially the area around Puteoli, was busy with the workshops of sculptors, potters, stuccoists, and painters. Late Republican Campania was one of the most active creative centers of the late Hellenistic world.

The area to the south and east of Vesuvius lay somewhat on the fringes of all this creative activity. It contributed to and profited from the general prosperity, and the latest contemporary artistic fashions were reflected on its walls. But its own interests were predominantly agricultural and its population, as the family names of Pompeii clearly show, was very largely Italic, many of the families being of Samnite origin but with a generous admixture of newcomers from other parts of Italy, reinforced in 80 B.C. by the establishment of colonies of Sullan veterans at Nola and Pompeii. Compared with Puteoli or Baiae Pompeii was perhaps a trifle provincial, and it lacked the Hellenic sophistication of Naples. Nevertheless, it was a prosperous and lively member of the Campanian community, at a moment when Campania was itself in the forefront of contemporary architectural and artistic progress.

Facing page:
**23**
**Head of a young man, perhaps a member of the Popidius family**
Fine-grained white marble, probably from Phrygia in Asia Minor
Height 36.5 cm
From the House of the Citharist (1, 4, 5), found together with No. 21 on 19 October 1868 in the stable block, having perhaps fallen from an upper room.

Rough surfaces on the shoulders mark the lines of drapery folds that have been dressed off, indicating that this was probably retrieved from a statue and adapted to a bust after the earthquake of A.D. 62. When found, the nose and ears were damaged and have been restored in plaster, but the repair to the lower lip was made in antiquity, in Italian marble. The hair was probably painted a reddish brown, and the slightly roughened surfaces of the eyeballs may have had the iris and pupil rendered in red and black in the manner usual at this period. The unusually smooth, transparent quality of the flesh surfaces is due to the fine marble, which also permitted the sculptor a greater subtlety and sensitivity of modeling than usual.

**17**
**Painted portrait of a man and his wife**
Height 65 cm, width 58 cm
From House VII, 2, 6, on the back wall of a small
*exedra* opening off the atrium

The man wears a toga and carries a papyrus
scroll with a red seal. His wife wears a tunic and
mantle, and her hair is dressed in a fashion popular about the middle of the first century A.D. In
her right hand she holds to her lips a *stylus* for
writing on the two-leaved wooden tablet spread
with wax which she holds in her left. Both in
style and in treatment there is a striking resem-
blance to the Egyptian mummy portraits of the
Roman period.

Facing page:
**19**
**Wall painting: figure of a girl**
Height 56 cm, width 38.5 cm
From Pompeii

The girl is probably intended to represent a figure
sacrificing or in attendance upon some religious
occasion.

## 18
**Wall painting: portrait of a woman in profile**
Height 52 cm, width 39 cm
From Herculaneum or Stabiae

Framed portrait from the center of the left-hand lateral panel of a Third Style wall. Old drawings of it show bands of ribbons hanging loosely down from the hair over the shoulders, and the loss of this overpainting accounts for the seeming disproportion of the neck. The same drawings indicate that the hair-band was shown as being made of some precious metal, and that from it sprang delicate sprays of flowers probably executed in pearls and emeralds on gold wire stems. The portrait itself is obviously imitating a cameo, and it has been suggested that it represents Cleopatra.

Facing page:
## 129
**Wall painting: Europa riding the bull**
Width 99 cm, height 125 cm
From the back wall of a *cubiculum* in the House of Jason (IX, 5, 18)

Third Style central panel portraying Europa, daughter of the King of Phoenicia, who, while playing on the seashore with her handmaidens, was approached by Zeus in the form of a white bull, which lured her into seating herself on its back and thereupon carried her off, across the sea to Crete. There, after bearing Zeus three sons, she married the King of Crete, who adopted her sons, one of whom, Minos, became his heir. The landscape, with its central oak tree (the tree sacred to Zeus), echoes the central scene.

On the left-hand wall of the same bedroom *(cubiculum)*, by the same hand, was the painting of Pan and the Nymphs (No. 114) and on the right-hand wall a painting of Hercules, Deianira, and the centaur Nessus. Common to all three paintings was the symbolic use of trees within the landscape.

**144, 145**
**Wall paintings: fantasy architecture from a Fourth Style wall**
Height 1.88 m, width 52 cm
From Pompeii, May 1760

Narrow vertical panels depicting slender fantasy architecture in receding perspective are commonly used to frame the central panel in one type of Fourth Style wall. On the broad plane surface of the central panel in the scheme from which these elements came was painted a small framed picture of Perseus and Andromeda (Naples Museum, inv. 8995), and in the middle of each lateral panel were roundels (see also Nos. 2, 141). One of these was the famous "Sappho" (Naples Museum, inv. 9084).

Facing page:
**114**
**Wall painting: Pan and the Nymphs**
Height 1.22 m, width 93 cm
From the left-hand wall of the same *cubiculum* in the House of Jason as No. 129

Third Style panel showing Pan, pipes in hand, seated on a rock with a goat at his feet. To the left are seated two Nymphs, one of them holding two reed pipes in her hand, while to the right another stands playing a lyre *(cithara)*. Beyond the left-hand Nymphs is a building set in a rocky landscape, central to which is a pine tree, sacred to Pan.

**111**
**Landscape panel of a rustic sanctuary**
Height 34 cm, length 61 cm
From Herculaneum

**150**
**Wall painting: woman giving water to a traveler**
Width 44 cm, height 38 cm
From the *tablinum* of the House of the
Dioscuri (VI, 9, 6)

The picture formed part of a longer landscape
frieze, with painted moldings top and bottom,
over the side panels of a Fourth Style wall.

Facing page:
**146**
**Wall painting: Theseus, slayer of the Minotaur**
Width 88 cm, height 97 cm
From the *exedra* off the peristyle in the House
of Gavius Rufus (VII, 2, 16)

The central panel of the left-hand wall of a
Fourth Style scheme. It shows Theseus victorious
from his battle with the Minotaur, the bull-
headed monster of Crete to whom the Athenians
had each year to send a tribute of youths and
maidens. The Minotaur lies dead in the entrance
to his lair, the Labyrinth, and his destined
victims press round Theseus in gratitude.

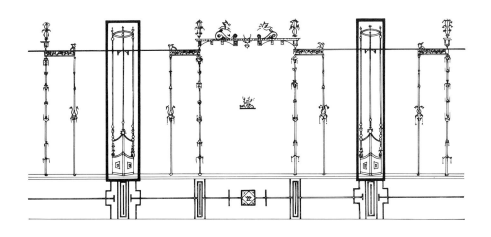

**115, 116**
**Wall paintings: pair of decorative details from a Third Style wall**
Height 2.00 m, width 44 cm
From Room 15 *(cubiculum)* in the Villa of
Agrippa Postumus at Boscotrecase, excavated
1903–1905

These are two of the vertical components of
the architectonic framework of the side walls
(see reconstruction) of which the dado was a
dark red and the rest of the background uni-
formly black. Though reminiscent of the
*candelabra* and tripod stands from which much
Third Style ornament was derived, they are here
reduced to a purely schematic, decorative form.
The detail is extremely delicate and includes small
sprays of foliage, now largely effaced, sprouting
from the vertical stems.

Facing page:
**135**
**Fragment of Fourth Style wall painting**
Width 98 cm, height 90 cm
From Pompeii

Fragment from the upper zone of an early
Fourth Style wall, including the upper border
and an *aedicula* set in a formal quasi-architec-
tural scheme of delicate garlands and slender
rods entwined with tendrils, reminiscent of fine
late Third Style work (as in the White Triclinium
in the House of M. Lucretius, IX, 3, 5). Within
the *aedicula* is the figure of a woman with flowing
draperies, poised as if flying.

80
**Wall painting of a garden** (detail)
Length 137 cm, height 32 cm
From Herculaneum

This scene, probably from the dado of a wall
of the late Third or Fourth Style, shows one
side of a garden enclosure, the trellised fence of
which is laid out symmetrically around three
semi-circular *exedrae*.

Most of the elements of this sort of fenced
garden are already present in the Garden
Room paintings from the Villa of Livia at Prima
Porta, and they recur in varying combinations
in many Pompeian paintings (see No. 79).

85
**Garden painting: a white stork and lizard and
a pet dog**
Length 1.30 m, height 55 cm
From the House of the Epigrams (v, 1, 18)

The painting stood in the southeast corner of
the peristyle, where it occupied a position closely
resembling that of the very similar paintings in
the peristyle of the House of the Menander.

**260-262**
**Three red pottery (terra sigillata) bowls**
Found in the *tablinum* of House VIII, 5, 9 on
4 October 1881, together with eighty-seven
others of the same forms and thirty-seven
pottery lamps, all packed in a wooden crate. The
bowls were made by several different Gaulish
potters.

**260**
Diameter 20.5 cm

Stamped in the center of the inside by the
maker Vitalis, who was active about A.D. 60–85.

**261**
Diameter 16 cm

Stamped as No. 260 but by Mommo, one of the
most prolific of South Gaulish potters.

**262**
Diameter 16.8 cm

The letters "MOM" were incised in the mold
in large cursive letters under the decoration,
probably by the potter Mommo (see No. 261).

**100**
**Small blue glass jug (askos)**
Height 11 cm, length 21.1 cm
From Pompeii, House IX, 2, 26

The glass-blower has imitated a shape long
familiar in Greek pottery and in Campanian
bronze ware.

**101**
**Small jug (askos) in black and white marbled
glass**
Height 9.5 cm, length 13.4 cm
From Pompeii, in IX, 7, 6

Like No. 100 this is free-blown, but it is squatter
in shape and made in thicker, opaque glass.

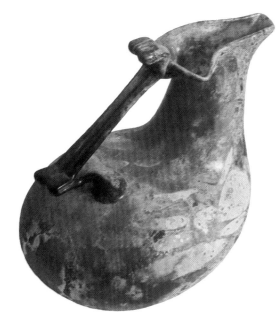

29

### 99
**Ribbed blue glass bowl**
Height 8.9 cm, diameter 18.9 cm
From Pompeii

These bowls were made by pressing soft glass
into a mold; the interior was polished on a wheel,
the exterior by a second, brief exposure to fire.
Bowls of this form, in multi-colored as well as
in monochrome glass, were popular in the first
century A.D.

### 104
**Dark blue glass jug**
Height 18 cm
From Pompeii

Fine-quality work, free-blown with a drawn-out
spout and an applied handle. The form clearly
imitates that of a bronze vessel.

### 98
**Stemmed goblet in cobalt blue glass**
Height 14 cm, diameter of rim 15.4 cm
From one of the sites in the Vesuvius area

The body was blown into a mold; two horizontal
wheel-cut lines decorate the outside. The stem is
formed from two large beads of glass and the foot
added separately. Such drinking cups were used
at table; for a silver version see No. 246.

**162**
**Gold lamp with two nozzles**
Height 15.1 cm, length 23.2 cm
From Pompeii

The design of lotus leaves was worked in relief
from the outside with a punch, after filling the
interior with pitch. The plain spouts and base
were cast separately and soldered into place. The
lid, now missing, would normally have been the
most highly decorated part.

**40**
**Gold bulla**
Length 6.5 cm, weight 14.08 grams
From the House of the Menander (1, 10, 4)

The *bulla,* a small bag-shaped amulet, was
worn around the neck, a practice the Romans
derived from the Etruscans, among whom it
seems to have been worn as an ornament by
both sexes. Among the Romans the gold *bulla*
(sometimes known as *Etruscum aureum*) took
on a more restricted significance, being worn
from infancy by the sons of citizens as a visible
token of free birth. On coming of age and formally assuming the dress of manhood (the *toga
virilis*), it was customary to lay the *bulla* cere-
moniously aside in the household *lararium* (see
No. 210). At a later date its use was permitted
also to the sons of freedmen.

31

**47**
**Gold armband in the form of a snake**
Diameter 8 cm, length 11 cm

One of a pair of armbands, each shaped from a
flat ribbon of gold on which the scales were
indicated with a V-shaped punch; the head was
cast separately, and the eyes were originally set
with green vitreous paste.

**50**
**Gold bracelet**
Diameter 8.3 cm
From House 1, 2, 3

Two lengths of thick gold wire loosely inter-
twined to form eight large loops, soldered
together at the crossings; over one of these is an
applied gold ornament.

**52**
**Part of a necklace of gold ivy leaves**
Length 53 cm
From Pompeii, 9 June 1877

The necklace consisted originally of two
concentric bands of ivy leaves stamped out of
sheet gold and linked to each other by tiny loops
of gold wire; the loops are masked by small gold
bosses. The 48 leaves of this piece converge
symmetrically upon a large convex gold disc. The
clasp that joined the two bands behind the neck
is missing.

# HISTORY OF POMPEII

*The town walls of Pompeii, originally built in the fifth century B.C. but repaired and heightened during successive crises (top: the Nola Gate; below: stretch of early masonry on the north wall)*

*Oscan inscription recording the building of the Samnite* Palaestra *(see page 87) in the later second century B.C. "Vibius Adiranus, son of Vibius, left money in his will to the men of Pompeii; with this money the quaestor of Pompeii, Vibius Vinicius, son of Maras, with the consent of the council had charge of the construction of this building and approved it"*

The earliest history of Pompeii must remain a matter of conjecture until the relevant archaeological levels have been more systematically explored. Finds made in the city's two Archaic sanctuaries, that of Apollo beside the Forum and of Hercules (the Doric Temple), show that by the sixth century B.C. Greek influence was very strong, and it may very well be that the site was actually first colonized by Greeks from Cumae, who recognized its advantages as a river-mouth station for trading with the native Italic agricultural communities of the Sarno valley. Pottery characteristic of the latter has been found in the same contexts, suggesting close association if not intermarriage with the local peoples; and Etruscan wares indicate commerce also with Etruscan Capua. From the outset the geographical position of Pompeii made it a meeting place of cultures.

The middle years of the fifth century, after the decisive defeat of the Etruscans in 474 by Cumae in alliance with Syracuse, were a period of Greek prosperity. The original 24-acre settlement of Pompeii on the spur overlooking the river mouth was at this time greatly enlarged, to include the whole area of some 160 acres enclosed by the surviving city walls. But the period of undisputed Greek authority was short-lived. The walls themselves were symptomatic of the threat from the hardy Italic tribesmen of the interior, who were already spilling down across the coastal plain. By the end of the century the entire Greek coastland, from Cumae in the north to Poseidonia (Paestum) in the south, had succumbed to the invaders: only Neapolis (Naples) managed to retain its independence.

The newcomers were part of a loose confederation of peoples, the Sabellians, who shared a common language called Oscan, a member of the same Indo-European group of languages as Latin. These peoples appear in the literature variously as Sabellians and as Samnites, from the name of the particular tribe around which resistance to Rome's southward advance was soon to crystallize; in the Sarno valley they merged with the Oscans, a closely related Italic tribe already settled in the coastal area. At the time intertribal disputes and alliances bulked large — it was one of these Sabellic tribes, the Campani of the area around Capua, who first called in the Romans in 343 B.C.; but seen in historical retrospect, the most important thing about them was the broad common heritage of Italic peasant culture and language they shared with each other and, at one remove, with the Romans. Without this common element the story of the union of central Italy under Roman rule would have been very different. Another gift these peoples shared with the Romans was that of taking on the externals of the more advanced peoples whom they conquered. The Greek component in the resulting mixed culture was to be a very important factor in the success story of Republican Campania.

During the Samnite wars, which ended in 290 B.C. with the establishment of Roman authority over the whole of central Italy, Pompeii was still a small country town. Its economy was predominantly agricultural, based on wine and oil, with some local industry, and supplemented by a flourishing commerce in wool and woolen goods. Such other importance as it had at this stage was as a harbor town for its more important neighbors Nola and Nuceria (Nocera) and for the smaller towns of the Sarno valley. But times were changing fast. The consolidation of Roman authority, the defeat of Carthage in the Second Punic War (218-201), and Rome's triumphant advance eastward into Greece, Asia Minor, and Syria opened up rich fields of economic enterprise of which the Campanians, with their mixed Graeco-Italic background, were ideally placed to take advantage. Puteoli (Pozzuoli) was now the principal port of Italy. Roman traders, prominent among them the Campanians, began to appear in large

The Amphitheater riot of A.D. 59
Naples Museum

numbers all over the eastern Mediterranean; and while a steadily increasing proportion of the financial capital was probably put up by wealthy Romans, there
were rich prizes for the Campanian merchants and middlemen and for those of
the Campanian landed gentry who had money to invest. By the second half of
the second century B.C. Pompeii was, as its monuments show, already a very
prosperous city.

The last century of the Roman Republic was a period of almost continuous
civil strife and deep social unrest, during which the political and economic
forces loosed by Rome's conquest of Italy, Carthage, and the Hellenistic king-
doms of the eastern Mediterranean battled their way to the new state of institu-
tional equilibrium that we call the Roman Empire. In such troubled times
Campania could not escape involvement: cities and individuals found themselves caught up in larger events, and many people lost their lives or property.
Pompeii itself was very far from being the happy small town without a history
that it is sometimes painted; but despite temporary ups and downs, it was still
able to maintain a surprising level of economic well-being. Because of its privileged economic position, Campania was better able than a great many parts of
Italy to adjust to the successive new situations, and when in 31 B.C. Caesar's
nephew and heir, Octavian (or Augustus, as he was to be known from 27 B.C.),
finally succeeded in reimposing peace and unified rule upon the Mediterranean
world, Pompeii was still a very prosperous town, well placed to take advantage
of the opportunities offered by the new Pax Romana.

From the earlier part of this period two closely related series of events stand
out as directly affecting the fortunes of Pompeii. One was the Social War of
90-89 B.C., in which Pompeii, with its fine walls, was one of the Campanian
strongholds of the Italian allies in their struggle to achieve full Roman citizen-
ship. There was heavy fighting, during which Herculaneum was occupied,
Stabiae captured and sacked, and Pompeii itself besieged by the future dictator,
Lucius Cornelius Sulla: one can still see the damage wrought by his artillery in
the walls near the Vesuvius Gate. We do not know the immediate local outcome

Graffito of a triumphant gladiator, drawn by a
Pompeian after the riot of A.D. 59: "Campani
(probably the inhabitants of a suburb of
Pompeii) you too were destroyed in the victory
over the Nucerians"

of those events, but the long-term result of the Social War was the unification of Italy south of the Po valley within the broad framework of the Roman polity.

The conclusion of the Social War did not, however, resolve the immediate local problems. It was left for Sulla to complete the Italian settlement after his return to Italy in 83 B.C. from Asia Minor at the head of a victorious army. Having eliminated all political opposition in Rome itself, he turned his hand to the larger problem with characteristic ruthlessness and efficiency. One of the most effective instruments to hand was the establishment of citizen colonies of loyal military veterans on land expropriated from past opponents. Many such colonies were planted in Campania, among them a group of possibly as many as two or three thousand families on the territory of Pompeii. It was a neat solution, satisfactory to all parties except the dispossessed, and, in extreme cases, it must have meant the virtual annihilation of the old Italic upper classes. At Pompeii, as we shall see, the long-term results were nothing like so drastic. But the immediate result was to give Pompeii and other similar colonies a new civic status, a new ruling class, and a new stake in the events of the world around them.

With the establishment of the Colonia Cornelia Veneria Pompeianorum in 80 B.C. we turn a page in the city's history. The historical perspectives shift, slightly but decisively. As a Hellenized Italic city Pompeii, though irrevocably involved in the fortunes of Roman Italy, had retained a certain measure of independence. Now, for better or for worse, she found herself a full partner in the great Roman adventure. For the next fifty years the death throes of the Roman Republic continued to offer the politically ambitious plenty of scope for direct involvement in larger events. We catch an occasional glimpse of such happenings in the pages of Cicero, who owned a property in the neighborhood: in 62 B.C. he successfully defended the founder of the colony, the dictator's relative Publius Cornelius Sulla, on a charge of involvement in the conspiracy of Catiline; in 49 B.C. Cicero himself, on his way to join Pompey in Greece, found himself approached by the commanders of the three cohorts stationed in or near the town (an offer he discreetly declined). Again, during the Servile War (73-71 B.C.), Spartacus' army remained for a long time in the countryside near Pompeii, and actually destroyed Pompeii's neighbor Nola. But such incidents were the inevitable by-products of troubled times. For the last century and a half of the city's existence, the inhabitants of Pompeii, in company with those of countless other colonies and municipalities in Italy, were fully engaged in reaping the material advantages of their new status.

From 80 B.C. onward the real history of Pompeii is that of the city and its inhabitants, and that can only be told in terms of the city's civic institutions, which are the subject of the section that follows. Here it must suffice to refer to the three remaining occasions on which Pompeii found itself front-page news outside Campania.

The first of these was the riot that took place in A.D. 59 after a gladiatorial spectacle in the Amphitheater, as a result of which a number of visiting spectators from Nuceria were killed or wounded. The matter reached the Senate in Rome, and as a punishment all spectacles in the Amphitheater were banned for a period of ten years—a sentence comparable today to a ten-year closure of the local football stadium. The scene is vividly portrayed in a contemporary picture, now in Naples Museum (see illustration), which was found in a house near the theater.

Then, on the fifth of February 62 there was a severe earthquake. Though

35

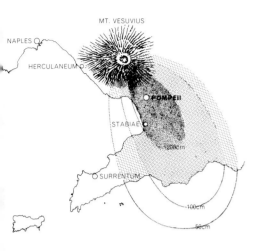

The area affected by the hail of pumice stones and the relative depths of ash ejected by Vesuvius in A.D. 79

nobody at the time knew it, this was Act One of the tragedy of A.D. 79, and like many earthquakes of a volcanic nature its effects were localized but intense, and Pompeii was the epicenter. The town was very badly damaged; quite how badly can be judged from the fact that when, seventeen years later, disaster hit again, only two of the city's public monuments (the Amphitheater and the Temple of Isis) and a handful of private houses had been completely restored. Of the Forum and the buildings around it, only in the Temple of Apollo was the work near completion; even allowing for the fact that after the eruption this whole area was ransacked for its metals, its marbles, and its building materials, it is quite evident that the only buildings where reconstruction work was not still in progress were those like the Capitolium, where it had not yet started—presumably because of plans to rebuild them in a more opulent, contemporary manner. In 79 the whole Forum area was a gigantic builders' yard. The same story is repeated all over the city: in the public bath buildings, the theaters, the Doric temple, the water supply, a great many of the private houses. As we shall see, this was not the only problem Pompeii was having to face in its last years, but the earthquake of 62 was in itself undoubtedly a major disaster.

The great eruption of Vesuvius of 24 August 79 came out of a clear sky. The volcano had been inactive since well before historical times and it was universally believed to be extinct. Villas and vineyards crowded up the slopes, and in a land where earthquakes are common the warning of A.D. 62 had passed unheeded.

For the course of the eruption, which followed a classic pattern, we have two contemporary sources: the analysis of the deposits of ash and cinders beneath which the whole city was buried, and the eyewitness account of Pliny the Younger, contained in two letters addressed to the historian Tacitus. At the time Pliny was staying with his uncle, the famous scientist and writer, who happened to be in command of the Roman fleet at Misenum, nineteen miles to the west, at the mouth of the Bay of Naples. It was about one o'clock in the afternoon when their attention was called to the cloud, shaped like a gigantic pine tree, which had appeared across the bay:

*I cannot describe its appearance and shape better than as resembling an umbrella pine tree, with a very tall trunk rising high into the sky and then spreading out into branches. I imagine this was because where the force of the blast was fresh it was thrust upwards, but as this lost impetus, or indeed as the weight of the cloud itself took charge, it began to thin out and to spread laterally. At one moment it was white, at another dark and dirty, as if it carried up a load of earth and cinders.*

(Pliny, *Letters* vi, 16)

Allied troops who witnessed the far less destructive eruption of March 1944 will at once recognize the description—nature's equivalent of the mushroom cloud released by an atomic bomb.

Summoning ships, the Elder Pliny headed straight for the coast near Herculaneum, where he found it already impossible to land. Instead he put in at Stabiae, at the coastal villa of a friend, Pomponianus, where he spent the night. In the small hours of the following morning a succession of violent earthquake shocks and the steadily falling ash drove the party down to the beach, where during the course of the morning of the 25th Pliny was overcome by the fumes and died. Meanwhile, Misenum was feeling the same earthquake shocks, and when a shift of wind into the east brought with it a cloud of darkness and falling ash the whole population took to the open countryside; it was not until the fol-

lowing day that the ashes began to cease falling and that a fitful daylight broke
through once more.

The eruption must have started between 10 and 11 o'clock on the morning
of the 24th, and by the evening of that day some 6 feet of ash had already fallen
on Pompeii. Here the first 8 or 9 feet of deposit consist of a thin scatter of lava
pebbles (*lapilli*), the debris of the plug of solidified basalt that had for so long
sealed the volcano, followed by successive layers of almost pure pumice. This
represents the body of volcanic magma that was ejected up the throat as soon as
it was clear, under conditions of great heat and enormous pressure, to a height
of several thousand meters (the trunk of the "pine tree"); on reaching the upper
atmosphere the drops of magma were able to expand, releasing some of the
gases they contained, and to fall as a dense, spreading cloud of incandescent,
gaseous pumice. More than two thirds of the deposits at Pompeii represent this
first, cataclysmic series of events, after which the gases of the interior were free
to escape upward with a much smaller admixture of pure magma, its place being
taken by increasing quantities of alien material, as the old volcanic matter of the
existing cone collapsed inward upon itself, causing a series of convulsive block-
ages and explosions. This was the peak moment of the eruption, involving a
tremendous release of gaseous pressure and causing the earthquakes that destroyed Pomponianus' villa at Stabiae and spread panic at Misenum. But although the deadly rain of gas and cinders continued, the body of actual solid
matter that fell was already tailing off rapidly. In terms of its power to destroy,
by the afternoon of the 25th the eruption had already done its worst.

The city of Pompeii had ceased to exist, buried beneath twelve feet of lethal
ash. We have no means of estimating the casualties, but in the town itself and the
immediate countryside they must have run into many thousands. Those who
got away did so in the first few hours, the lucky ones by sea, the rest striking inland before the roads were blocked and the air became unbreathable. Those who
dallied to collect their valuables or who took shelter in the houses and cellars
died miserably, some when the roofs and upper stories collapsed upon them
under the weight of the ash, most of them suffocated by the steady accumulation
of deadly, sulphurous fumes. The ash solidified around their bodies, leaving for
posterity the pathetic record of their death agonies amid the darkness of that
terrifying August day.

When something like normality had been restored a commission was sent to
Campania to report, but there was nothing to be done. Herculaneum and many
of the villas of the coast along the foot of Vesuvius had vanished from sight beneath an engulfing torrent of volcanic mud, washed down the mountainside by
the torrential rains that accompanied the eruption. Pompeii and Stabiae were
slightly better off in that the upper parts of many of the taller buildings were still
visible above the mantle of ash. Here it was at least possible to do some salvage.
The Forum area was ransacked for its bronze statues and its fine building materials, and many houseowners — and others — grubbed their way down into the
houses, hunting for strongboxes and caches of valuables. But the town was
beyond resurrection. The survivors drifted away or were settled elsewhere and,
as has happened many times in Campanian history, nature took over and what
had been Pompeii became once more rich agricultural land. The knowledge that
there had once been a town here lingered on in folk memory: in the eighteenth
century the area was still known as Città (*civitas,* or "city"). But as far as the
learned world was concerned Pompeii, like Herculaneum, had been wiped off
the map and had laboriously to be rediscovered.

# THE TOWN:
# GOVERNMENT AND PEOPLE

*Poster painted on the wall of House III, 2, 1, advertising gladiatorial games to be given at the expense of Lucretius Satrius*

*Lucius Caecilius Felix, father of Lucius Caecilius Jucundus Naples Museum*

*Marcus Holconius Rufus Naples Museum*

A great deal of our information about life in Pompeii is derived from inscriptions. In addition to the ordinary everyday uses of writing that distinguish any advanced society, the Romans seem to have had a strong portion of the common human passion for self-commemoration. Three main categories of inscriptions may be distinguished. One is that of formal monumental epigraphy on stone or bronze, ranging from long, elaborate, formal texts down to the simple tombstones of the domestic slave and his family. To this category belong dedications to divinities and records of religious events; inscriptions in honor of members of the Imperial family and distinguished citizens; building inscriptions and funerary inscriptions. A second category is that of the inscriptions used in commerce and private life to denote the source of ownership of certain goods, or to facilitate accounting. These might be an integral part of the object inscribed, as were the maker's stamps on many sorts of pottery or lamps, or they might be scratched or painted on the object, as frequently for example on silver ware or the painted tally marks on amphoras. A third group, in which by the circumstances of its destruction Pompeii is unusually rich, is that of *graffiti* (literally "scratches"), a term that may be used to denote any sort of ephemeral sign or text scratched or painted on plaster or other appropriate surfaces. Many of these are the work of the inevitable idle scribbler, but a very unusual and important group consists of electoral posters painted on the fronts of the houses of the candidates or their supporters (see page 41). The evidence is not evenly spread: for the final period of the city we have a great deal of electoral propaganda, but few formal inscriptions setting out the names and careers of the successful candidates. Even so, as a Who's Who to the personalities of local politics it remains an invaluable source of information.

Another unusual group of inscriptions is that of the *tabulae ceratae,* the wax-surfaced wooden tablets upon which a local banker, Lucius Caecilius Jucundus, kept his business records. These were buried in the earthquake of 62 and never recovered; and not only do they throw light on aspects of contemporary life about which we normally hear very little, but they tell us a lot about the people involved. Because of the rigid rules of precedence prevailing in Roman society, even a list of witnesses can be an eloquent document.

Most of these inscriptions record the names of individuals, a great many of them in some public capacity, and to understand their significance it will be helpful at this point to glance briefly at the Roman rules governing the use of names, which fortunately for us were remarkably precise. By the end of the Republic it was standard practice for a Roman citizen to bear three names. Thus the full name of the most distinguished citizen of Augustan Pompeii was M[arcus] Holconius M[arci] f[ilius] Rufus. His middle name, Holconius, was that of the *gens,* the family of which he was a member, the equivalent of a modern surname. His first name (*praenomen*) was given to him at birth, and in normal Roman practice it was written in abbreviated form (A. for Aulus, L. for Lucius, Gn. for Gnaeus, etc.) and in official documents a man would normally also give his father's *praenomen*, which in the case of Holconius Rufus was the same as his own. In early Republican times two names had sufficed; but a developed society can carry only a limited number of plain John Smiths, and quite early it became the practice in aristocratic circles to add a third name, or *cognomen,* a practice that spread steadily down the social scale to all levels of citizen society. These *cognomina,* when first adopted, were very commonly descriptive (*Ahenobarbus,* "Brazenbeard"; *Calvus,* "Baldhead"; *Faventinus,* "from Faventia" [modern Faenza]), but they very soon became conventional names that ran in families. M. Holconius Rufus ("Redhead") was no more necessarily himself red-headed than his brother Celer ("Swift") was fast-moving. To his friends he was probably known as Rufus, although on this point there were no hard and fast rules. Cicero was M. Tullius Cicero, but Pliny the Elder was Caius Plinius Secundus, while his nephew on his sister's side, Publius Caecilius Secundus, whom he adopted, became Caius Plinius Caecilius Secundus (taking on his adopted father's family name but retaining his own [Caecilius] as a *cognomen*).

Women used a simpler form of the same system, usually at this period just their family name together with that of the father or husband whose legal dependents they were, while household slaves carried a single name, which was normally Greek, a convention that reflects the fact that the overwhelming majority of such slaves were of Greek-speaking extraction. Slaves, it must be remembered, were members of the family. If they were given their freedom (see below) they took their former master's name and forename, usually retaining their own slave name as a *cognomen*. A hypothetical slave of M. Holconius Rufus, named Narcissus, would have become officially M. Holconius M[arci] l[ibertus = freedman] Narcissus, whereas the son of the latter would have been (say) M. Holconius M. f[ilius] Primus, born free and from his name indistinguishable from any other freeborn citizen. There were innumerable possible nuances of the system, and with the passage of time names tended to become more complex and many fresh names came into circulation. But down to A.D. 79 the main rules still broadly applied.

From the inscriptions we learn that M. Holconius Rufus had been a *duovir* of the colony five times (the fourth time in 2/1 B.C.) and *quinquennalis* twice; he was a *flamen Caesaris Augusti;* he was an official patron of the colony; and he was one of the three known Pompeians to have been appointed a *tribunus militum a populo,* an honorary office that gave him equestrian rank in Rome, a position of privilege second only to senatorial rank. Together with his brother, Celer, he modernized the Large Theater after the model of the Theater of Marcellus in Rome. This was a very distinguished municipal career. What did these titles signify, and how did the system work?

When a Roman colony was founded it was given its own written constitution and, because the Romans were an orderly minded people, such constitutions tended to follow a broadly uniform pattern, with relatively minor variations to meet special local circumstances. There is no direct record of the law with which in 80 B.C. Sulla established the Colonia Cornelia Veneria Pompeianorum, but we do have fragments of several other late Republican or early Imperial constitutions, and it is evident that that of Pompeii followed conventional lines.

The colony was established initially by an official (*deductor*) who was appointed by the central government and who in this case was the dictator's relative, Publius Cornelius Sulla. His tasks included the appropriation and allocation of lands for the new settlers, the establishment of a municipal council, and the appointment of the first body of magistrates. The council, a body usually of some 80-100 members, was known corporately as the *ordo decurionum* and its individual members as decurions (*decuriones*). Decurions had to be freeborn citizens; certain professions were ineligible (an odd list, including innkeepers, auctioneers, comedy actors, gravediggers, gladiators, trainers) and others (shopkeepers and small traders) eligible only under conditions that at this date would have been prohibitive; tenure was for life, unless a holder was specifically disqualified for some breach of the conditions; and — a very important provision — there was a high property qualification. A decurion, and *a fortiori* a magistrate,

M HOLCONIVM
PRISCVM·II·VIR·I·D· POMARI·VNIVERSI CVM·H·FLVIOVESTALE·ROG

was expected to spend money on the community. The *ordo* in effect constituted a moneyed municipal aristocracy, and as long as money was plentiful membership was a valued privilege. It was a Roman senate in miniature, but— as Cicero remarks to a friend who had asked his support in getting his stepson appointed to the *ordo* of Pompeii—it was rather harder to get into.

The senior elected magistrates were a pair of *duoviri,* who between them presided over the meetings of the *ordo,* handled all important financial business, and administered local justice. Among other privileges certain senior priesthoods were reserved for members of the duoviral families, and a magistrate with good connections at the imperial court might aspire to the honorary but prestigious position of *patronus.* The *duoviri* were supported by a pair of junior magistrates, aediles, who dealt with such day-to-day administrative matters as the maintenance of streets and public buildings, the management of markets, and the issue of licenses and permits. These were young men at the beginning of their careers, and since election to a magistracy carried with it membership in the *ordo,* there was no shortage of candidates. Every five years the *duoviri* had special powers and were known as *quinquennales,* with the special task of carrying out a municipal census and of reviewing the qualifications of the members of the *ordo.* This last power must have greatly reinforced the tendency for municipal power to fall into the hands of a small self-perpetuating group of wealthy families. Only if things went badly wrong was central authority (i.e., from the time of Augustus onward, the emperor) likely to intervene. A properly qualified newcomer could in theory seek popular election, but in practice the only sure access was through marriage or adoption into the ruling families and the best key to that door was wealth.

The magistrates were elected annually by the whole body of free citizens, who were for the purpose divided into voting districts. As the electoral propaganda shows (most of it admittedly from the last period of the town's history, when the hold of the old families had largely broken down) this was a duty that the population entered into with gusto; and while many of the supporters were no doubt simply friends, neighbors, and clients of the candidates, others were organized bodies that may be presumed to have had a serious economic or social interest in the outcome. Religious associations such as the *Isiaci* and the *Venerii,* influential trade associations such as the fullers (*fullones*), bodies of people involved in agriculture or transport, the fishermen, the bakers, the goldsmiths, various sorts of small shopkeepers or stallholders, all of these are attested, together with a number of other groups of a less serious character—"the draughtsplayers," "the theatergoers," "the late drinkers," and so on. Elections were evidently lively affairs.

There were also a number of organizations of a partly administrative, partly social or religious character (the distinction is not always an easy one to draw), which offered an outlet to citizens or other residents who were not qualified to become ordinary magistrates. It has to be remembered that there were also substantial groups of resident foreigners. But although, slave or freeborn, a man's position was rigidly defined by his civil status, this was also a surprisingly fluid society. Not only could slaves of ability rise to positions of very considerable responsibility as stewards, bailiffs, managers of large estates, and the like, but slavery was actually one of the recognized roads to social advancement. A Roman citizen had the right of bestowing freedom upon any slave who had given faithful service, a right that was freely exercised; and although a freedman, or *libertus,* was debarred from holding certain positions that called for free birth, his children born after he obtained his freedom were the equals at law of any other Roman citizen.

A great many of the domestic slaves came from the Greek-speaking East as prisoners of war, as the victims of a flourishing slave trade along and across the frontiers, or even as children sold into slavery by their families. Many of them had natural abilities and aptitudes in fields where the Romans were by temperament and position less qualified, and by the first century A.D. a very high percentage of the professional and commercial skills of a town like Pompeii were in their hands, either as trusted slaves working for their masters, or else as freedmen operating on their own behalf or as agents of their former masters. Doctors, teachers, accountants, secretaries, architects, decorators, barbers, cooks, small craftsmen and tradesmen of every sort, the overseers and technicians of commerce and industry, the staffs of the city offices: by the first century A.D. almost all of these would have been slaves or descendants of slaves, and, because of their natural ability and training, many of them were well-to-do and some of them were very wealthy. Trimalchio, the millionaire freedman of Petronius' *Satyricon,* is a caricature, but he is a caricature that everybody would have recognized as drawn from life.

It was, as we have seen, the regular practice for a freedman to adopt his former master's family name, and by the second generation it is often quite impossible to distinguish the descendants of freedmen from members of the parent family. Statistics elude us, but by A.D. 79 a very substantial proportion of the free urban population of Pompeii must have been descended from freedmen, and in many cases from the freedmen of freedmen. (In the countryside the proportion would have been less.) Much of the economy of the town was in their hands, and many of them were socially ambitious. The election posters of the last period include a lot of the old names, and although some of these were doubtless still the lineal descendants of the old Samnite and Roman families, a great many others were unquestionably the second- and third-generation products of this extraordinary ethnic melting pot.

For a vivid glimpse of the system at work we may turn to the inscription recording the rebuilding of the Temple of Isis after the earthquake of 62. The restoration was paid for by N. Popidius Celsinus, who bears the name of one of the most distinguished of the pre-Roman families of Pompeii, the Popidii. It must have cost a lot of money, at a time when the town was in serious financial difficulties, and in return the council was doubtless glad to elect him to their number. The only surprising feature is that at the time Popidius was a boy of six. The truth is, of course, that the real donor was the boy's father, N. Popidius Ampliatus, who happened to have been born a slave and who, being himself debarred from membership in the *ordo,* chose instead to buy his son's way into it. But for the eruption, Celsinus, with his family's wealth behind him, might well in due course have become the town's chief magistrate.

*Inscription from the Temple of Isis (no. 10)*
*Naples Museum*

The case of the restoration of the Temple of Isis is obviously in some respects exceptional, but it illustrates admirably the intent behind the system. Without doing violence to the inherited Roman prejudices in favor of free birth and against most forms of direct commercial activity, a real effort was made to engage the loyalties of the socially underprivileged and to direct their energies and wealth into socially useful channels. One such outlet was in the local administration of the *vici* and *pagi,* the subdistricts into which the town and its territory were divided (see p. 92). There were bodies known as *ministri,* who were mostly freedmen, but who might include freeborn citizens and in some cases even slaves. In origin the duties of the *ministri* may have been mainly religious, but, as organized bodies, they constituted a useful peg on which to hang other local responsibilities; they carried status, and we find them contributing financially to such municipal enterprises as building and the provision of games. Another important outlet was provided by the institution of the imperial cult in the time of Augustus (see p. 86). Here again, although the forms were ostensibly religious, the objectives were in reality far wider. The *Augustales* in particular were recruited from the most prominent freedmen of the community. They ranked immediately after the members of the *ordo* and, in addition to a large statutory payment on election, they were expected to use their wealth liberally on behalf of the community. In A.D. 79 the golden age of the *Augustales* was still to come, but even so they were already a powerful force within the community.

At Pompeii as nowhere else outside Rome we can follow the issues of local politics in terms of the individuals directly involved, the man in the street as well as the candidate for whom he voted. We must be content, however, to summarize the broad conclusions that emerge from the study of this mass of detailed information, insofar as it illustrates the history of the town during the 160 years of its existence as a Roman colony.

The first fifty years (80-31 B.C.), as reflected in the names of those who held municipal office or who were candidates for office, were closely influenced by the play of events elsewhere in Rome and Italy: the shifts of power and of allegiance in Rome itself following the rise of Caesar and, striking deeper and more lastingly, the breakup of the old tribal Italy and the steady emergence of a more urbanized, more broadly based Roman Italy. In this respect the founder of the colony, P. Cornelius Sulla, seems to have acted with considerable statesmanship and foresight. Although the colony was in intention founded as a closed electoral society from which the old Samnite families were excluded, within barely a generation we find members of the latter already back in the *ordo,* and they were joined there by an increasing number of families from other parts of Campania or from the impoverished inland districts of central Italy. The pattern is a familiar one. The product of a society that was out of balance, with large sections of the population adrift socially and seeking fresh opportunities within the enduring framework of Italian geography, there are many analogies with modern times.

If the first fifty years were, therefore, a time of rather rapid change, the next sixty to seventy years were characterized by a no less remarkable stability. Toward the end of the previous period many of the newcomers seem to have been partisans of the future emperor Augustus, and with the firm establishment of central authority after his victory at Actium in 31 B.C. they found themselves very comfortably placed. For a couple of generations the control of Pompeii seems to have lain in the hands of the small group of closely interrelated families to which M. Holconius Rufus and his brother belonged. As large landed pro-prietors, with profitable outlets in wine production, the tile industry, and sheep farming, much of the local economy was in their hands: their wealth is attested by the sums they spent on buildings, games, and other municipal amenities, and they had secured an almost complete monopoly of civic office. Because of their close ties with central authority — the establishment of the imperial cult and the institution of the *Augustales* are symptomatic — it was a period during which any lingering Campanian eccentricities (for example, the use of the old Samnite weights and measures) were quietly eliminated. As the ferment of the Civil Wars settled, the processes of Romanization begun in 80 B.C. came to fruition. By the death of Augustus' successor, Tiberius, in A.D. 37, Pompeii was as fully Roman a city as were Mantua, Sulmona, and Venusia (Venosa, in Apulia), the birthplaces of Vergil, Ovid, and Horace.

The last forty-odd years of the city's history were by contrast a period of change and of urban crisis. The earthquake of A.D. 62 was a serious aggrava-tion of a difficult situation; another must have been the loss of imperial favor after the Amphitheater riot of A.D. 59. But the underlying causes were political and economic. For one thing, Italy in general and Campania in particular were beginning to lose out economically to some of the developing provinces over-seas; for another, the monopoly of wealth formerly exercised by the old landed classes was facing ever-increasing competition from the emergent middle class to which the wealthy freedmen belonged. Exactly how the crisis developed and on whose authority it was resolved we do not know. There are signs of imperial intervention (the normal procedure when the affairs of a municipality got out of hand) and perhaps of a temporary suspension of the normal civic institutions during the forties. It is not until after the adoption of Nero by his stepfather, the emperor Claudius, in A.D. 50, that we begin once more to find records of ap-pointments to the normal magistracies and priesthoods. But from then on the record is extensive, and the message is clear. It shows that there had been an almost complete break with the recent past and with the group of families that had virtually controlled the city for more than half a century. Instead, many of the office-holders of the last period are from families with no previous political record; others are from old families that had long been excluded from office, and yet others are manifestly of freedman descent.

The monopoly of local authority by the established landed families had gone, and its place was being taken by a society in which privilege and wealth were more widely spread, but which found it difficult to fill the gap left by the with-drawal of the old, comfortable municipal paternalism. Pompeii was still a busy city, but it had fewer resources. It is no accident that in A.D. 79, seventeen years after the earthquake, only two major public buildings had been completely restored or that many of the fine old houses were being subdivided and con-verted into commercial premises. Another generation, and a great deal more of the older, wealthier Pompeii would have vanished. If it was the city's destiny to be preserved for posterity as a monument to a way of life, the eruption of 79 came just in time.

# THE TOWN: PLANNING AND ARCHITECTURE

The early history of Pompeii is faithfully reflected in its town plan. The original settlement, which occupied the southwest corner of the later town, was situated on a spur of higher ground, projecting from the lower slopes of Vesuvius and looking out over the mouth of the river Sarno and the Bay of Naples. It was defended by a circuit of walls that on the south and west sides followed the cliffs above the river mouth, and on the landward side faced out across the saddle that carried the coast road from Naples toward Stabiae and the Sorrento peninsula, following a curving line still clearly visible in the street plan of the later town. Within this circuit the early town was laid out on orderly, though not mathematically precise, lines. Of the early buildings, the positions of two can be established: the sanctuary of Apollo, which lay beside the reserved open space that was later to become the Forum, and that of Hercules (?), finely situated on a rocky spur that projected southeastward above the river (later the "Triangular Forum"), possibly outside the city walls. This early settlement covered some twenty-four acres, and the population is estimated at about 2,000 to 2,500 people.

With its command of local land and river traffic and its ready access to the sea, the settlement prospered and grew rapidly, and in the fifth century B.C. it was greatly enlarged northward and eastward, within a new circuit of defensive walls enclosing a roughly oval area of some 160 acres. These walls, several times strengthened and repaired, were to remain the effective boundary of the city throughout its subsequent history: any subsequent expansion (and the inscriptions and excavation confirm that there was such expansion) was into suburban areas outside the gates.

The new town was laid out in the Greek manner. This consisted ideally of long, narrow, rectangular residential blocks separated by narrow access-streets *(stenōpoi)* running at right angles to the main traffic avenues *(plateai)*, and it can be seen at its simplest and most orthodox in the area south of the Via dell'Abbondanza, toward the Amphitheater. Elsewhere there are many irregularities of layout, but all of them make good sense as a rationalization of the already existing road-system outside the walls of the early settlement: the main coast road running southeastward from the Herculaneum Gate and down the well-marked valley that led to the Stabian Gate; and, radiating outward, a web of roads heading for Naples and Herculaneum, the farms on the slopes of Vesuvius, Nola, and Stabiae and Nuceria. With a little tidying up at important intersections, it is all there, a classic instance of an orderly planning system superimposed upon an existing topographical situation in such a way as to cause a minimum of disruption to established suburban street frontages and property rights.

Of the architecture of the earliest town we have little more than the scanty remains of the two Greek temples, including the platform of one of them and a selection of the gaily painted terracotta architectural ornament that once covered the superstructures of both. The earliest substantial surviving structures belong to the turn of the fourth and third century B.C., and it is not really until the last century of Samnite rule, in the second century B.C., that we begin to get any coherent picture of the town as such. At this time there was still plenty of room: among the several wealthy houses of the period still standing in A.D. 79 was the House of the Faun, which occupied an area of some six acres, covering a whole city block. During this period there was also a lot of public building. The Forum was enlarged and monumentalized by the addition of enclosing porticoes; at the north end it was dominated by a large, upstanding temple of Jupiter, and off the southwest corner there now opened a grandiose new basilica.

# Pompeii

The original settlement at Pompeii

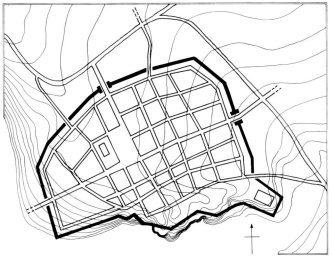

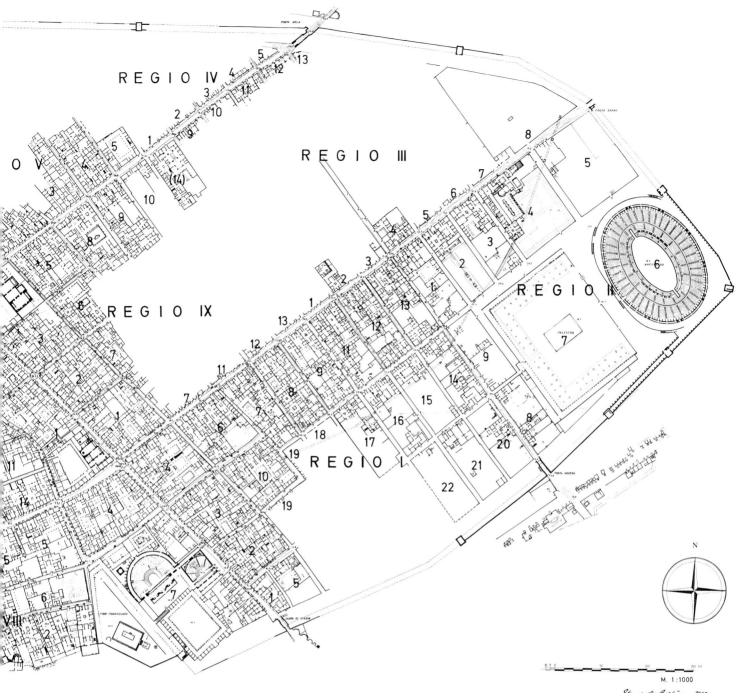

PORTA NOLA

REGIO IV

REGIO III

PORTA SARNO

O V

REGIO IX

REGION

PALESTRA
7

ANFITEATRO
6

REGIO I

PORTA NOCERA

VIII

FORO TRIANGOLARE

PORTA DI STABIA

VII

N

M. 1:1000

Stand der Grabungen 1969
H. Eschebach del.

Map of Pompeii
Courtesy of Hans Eschebach

47

1. Forum
2. Temple of Venus
3. Forum Baths
4. House of the Tragic Poet
5. House of Sallust
6. Villa of Diomedes
7. Villa of the Mysteries
8. Temple of Fortuna Augusta
9. House of the Faun
10. Insula VI, 13
11. House of the Vettii
12. House of the Gilded Amorini
13. Fullery
14. House of the Silver Wedding
15. Central Baths
16. House of the Centenary
17. Bakery of Modestus
18. Stabian Baths
19. Temple of Isis
20. Theaters (see p. 87)
21. House of the Menander
22. Caupona of Euxinus
23. House of the Ship "Europa"
24. House of Julius Polybius
25. House of Pinarius Cerialis
26. House of "Loreius Tiburtinus"
27. "Praedia" Julia Felix
28. Palaestra

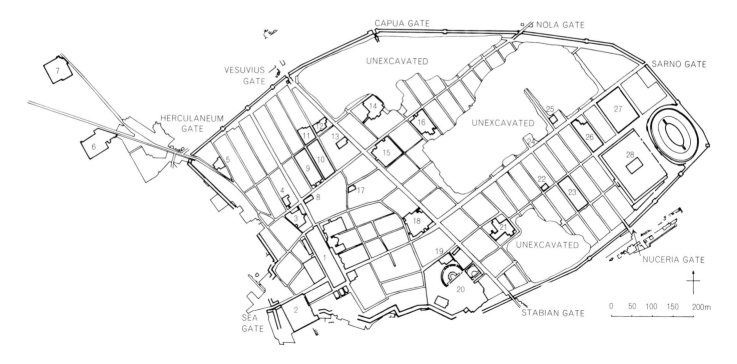

*Aerial view of the Forum from the
south, showing also the houses
terraced out over the town walls.*

## The Forum

1. *Temple of Jupiter*
2. *Provisions market (macellum)*
3. *Sanctuary of the City Lares*
4. *Temple of Vespasian*
5. *Cloth traders hall (Eumachia Building)*
6. *Voting hall (comitium)*
7. *Chief magistrates' (duovirs') office*
8. *Council chamber*
9. *Junior magistrates' (aediles') office*
10. *Basilica*
11. *Temple of Apollo*
12. *Control of weights and measures*
13. *Cereals market*
14. *Commemorative arches*

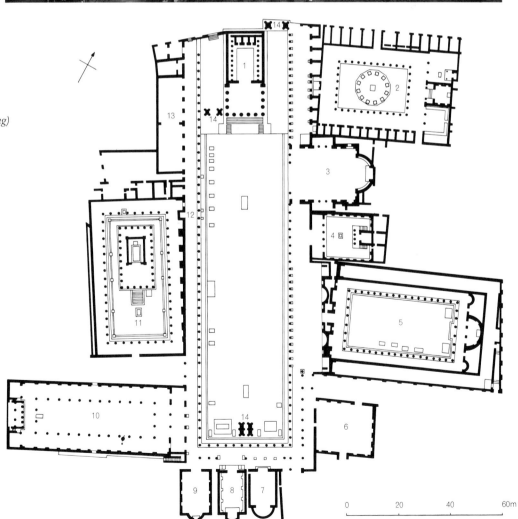

49

To this same period belong also the first bath buildings of the new Roman type, the Large Theater in its original form, the elegant Doric colonnades of the Triangular Forum, and, very probably, the predecessors of such later temples as those of Venus, of Zeus Meilichios, and of Isis. Typical of this late Samnite-period architecture are the use of the brown tufa stone of Nocera, especially for house frontages, and of the First Style ("Masonry Style") painted stucco ornament to cover all the more important interior wall surfaces.

Although the establishment of the Sullan colony in 80 B.C. was achieved without any radical change to the existing urban structure, it was, as one would expect, followed by considerable building activity. The city walls were repaired; the temple at the head of the Forum was rebuilt and rededicated in honor of the Roman Capitoline triad, Jupiter, Juno, and Minerva; the Stabian Baths were enlarged and modernized; and a number of new public buildings were erected, including a smaller, covered theater *(theatrum tectum)* beside the existing open-air theater, an amphitheater (inaugurated in 70 B.C.) and a second public bath building, near the Forum. The list is an interesting one, illustrating as it does not only the initial contribution of the new colonists, but also their rapid assimilation to local ways. For all its top-dressing of Roman colonial forms, Pompeii was still a Campanian city.

Full Romanization came only under Augustus and his immediate successors, a process neatly symbolized by the formal adoption of the Roman system of weights and measures in place of the old Sabellian system, which the Sullan colony had retained. Once again, however, it was a process of organic development and mutual assimilation within the existing framework rather than one of radical change. The Forum was progressively modernized by the addition of a meat and fish market *(macellum)*, a group of city offices, and a voting precinct; by the construction of the "Eumachia Building" by the patroness of the most powerful of the city's trade associations, the wool merchants; and by the rebuilding in limestone of the Forum porticoes—this last still in progress at the time of the earthquake of A.D. 62. Other major public works of this period include provision for the newly established imperial cult; the creation of a huge exercise ground *(palaestra)* near the Amphitheater; an elaborate remodeling of the old Samnite-period theater, undertaken by the wealthy brothers Holconius (see p. 40) in conscious imitation of the Augustan Theater of Marcellus in Rome; and the building of an aqueduct and a city-wide system of public water points. To this same period, between 80 B.C. and the middle of the first century A.D., belong most of the large private houses, with their elaborate schemes of Second and Third Style painted decoration. Both in the public and the private sector, this was a time of great and varied architectural activity.

By contrast, the last thirty years before the eruption were a time of economic stress and of gathering urban crisis. After the earthquake many of the large private houses were abandoned as residences; seventeen years later only two public monuments (the Amphitheater and the Temple of Isis) had been completely restored and there was little or no new public building. In 79 the Forum was a vast builder's yard, and even the water supply was still under repair. Of the few exceptions, the building usually identified as a public *lararium,* in honor of the city's protecting divinities, and the small temple in honor of Vespasian, could both have been considered necessary acts of propitiation toward religious and secular authority, following the disaster of A.D. 62. The only major new project of a utilitarian nature was a large new bath building, the Central Baths, still incomplete in A.D. 79.

*A street in Pompeii (The paving stones are made of hard gray lava.)*

In its use of building materials and construction techniques the architecture of Pompeii lies rather on the fringes than at the center of contemporary Italian building history — rather surprisingly so when one considers that the event that changed the face of classical architecture, the discovery of the unique properties of the mortar based on the volcanic sand of west central Italy, took place little more than 20 miles away, at Puteoli (Pozzuoli), and that some of the outstanding early manifestations of its use are still to be seen at Baiae. At Pompeii there was evidently a considerable prejudice in favor of the familiar Greek construction traditions still to be overcome. It was only in such frankly innovating building types as the amphitheater and the bath building that the arch and the vault (the forms in which the new Roman "concrete" found its ideal expression) could be used freely and explicitly without doing violence to the conventions of established monumental taste. Viewed in context, the amphitheater in particular appears as one of the outstanding early examples of the emergence of an architectural aesthetic based on the candid exploitation of the visual properties of the arch. At the time this was something quite new in classical architecture.

Another conspicuous innovation, in this case well represented at Pompeii, was the emergence during the last two centuries B.C. of a number of the new building types that were to figure so prominently in the later history of Roman architecture. Pompeii, though surely not a major creative center in its own right, was in this respect right in the mainstream of progressive architectural thinking. The stone-built Amphitheater, the upstanding Roman-type theater, the Basilica, the bath building, the market building with a circular pavilion of the type here represented beside the Forum: all of these important and distinctive architectural types seem first to have taken monumental shape in southern Italy rather than in Rome itself, and to have been products of the new social needs and opportunities created by Roman wealth and power operating within a setting of sophisticated local building skills and technical know-how. Although the amphitheater as an institution came from central Italy, Rome itself did not have a permanent amphitheater building until 29 B.C.; the first permanent theater in the capital dates from 55 B.C. and the first public bath building not before 19 B.C. There had been a basilica, the Basilica Porcia, beside the Roman Forum as early at 184 B.C.; but even in this case there is good reason to believe that the prototype came from South Italy, and the Basilica beside the Forum at Pompeii is the earliest example surviving anywhere. In this respect Campania during the second and first centuries B.C. was fertile soil, and by the accident of its preservation Pompeii offers us a unique vision of Imperial Roman architecture in the making.

# THE POMPEIAN HOUSE
# AND GARDEN

No survey of the art of Pompeii can be complete without some knowledge of the wealthy houses in which so much of it found its natural place. Buildings such as the House of the Faun, the House of the Menander, and the House of the Vettii figured as prominently in the local artistic life of their time as they do today in the itinerary of the modern visitor. They were not, of course, the only type of urban dwelling. There were many small, simpler family houses; there were modest upper-story apartments, particularly in the later period; and there were one-room or two-room *tabernae* that opened directly off the street, and served both as workshops and as living quarters for the poorest families. But, given the family-centered nature of traditional Italic society, the large, well-to-do houses did in fact bulk far larger than their equivalents would do in any advanced modern society, or indeed in the later urban architecture of Rome itself; the owners of these houses constituted the major source of patronage for local artistic enterprise.

As an architectural form the Pompeian house was very much a phenomenon of its age and place, occupying a midway position between the great hall of archaic Italic practice and the luxurious town residences of the wealthy Roman families of the Imperial age. Like any such term, "the Pompeian house" represents an abstraction, a convenient label for a page of architectural history torn from what was in fact a continuously developing historical narrative: but the use of this term may be justified by the strong element of formal continuity that runs right through the three centuries and more separating the earliest from the latest surviving examples. It does, moreover, greatly simplify description. Although by the end of the period the names and functions of some of the rooms were changing or had become obsolete (as in our own times such names as "parlor," "powder room," and "cloak room"), it is still broadly possible to use the same terminology to describe the individual members of the whole series.

As late as the early second century B.C. a typical Pompeian atrium house such as the House of Sallust (VI. 2, 4) was still essentially an inward-facing building, enclosed by bare walls and lit almost exclusively from within. The dominant feature of the plan was a large centrally lit hall, the *atrium*, the roof of which might in earlier times still have taken on one of the several forms described by later writers, although by the second century B.C. it seems invariably to have been of "compluviate" form, sloping downward and inward toward a rectangular opening (*compluvium*) situated above a rectangular basin (*impluvium*), so as to admit more light and at the same time to replenish the cisterns that were the house's principal water supply.

Grouped around the atrium were the other rooms of the house. The entrance was originally set back within an entrance porch (*vestibulum*) beyond which lay a short corridor (*fauces*). To right and left were service rooms (in the House of Sallust their place was already taken by shops facing outward onto the street), and along the two longer sides of the atrium itself a series of small, square bed-chambers (*cubicula*), in which the position of the couch was usually marked by the pattern of the floor and often also by the shape of the ceiling. Along the fourth side two lateral wings (*alae*) extended outward, giving access to a range of rather larger rooms. In the center, opposite the entrance and structurally open toward the main hall, from which it could be closed off by a wooden screen or a curtain, lay the *tablinum*. This was the principal reception room of the house and, unlike most of the other rooms, it was often lit by a window, which opened onto the garden plot (*hortus*) beyond. Of the two rooms on either side of it, one was often used as a dining room or *triclinium*, so named from the ⊓-shaped

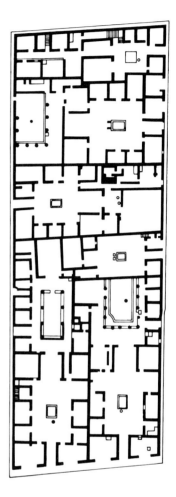

*A typical residential insula (city block)* VI, 13

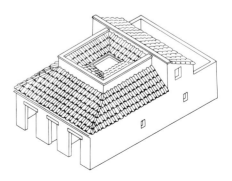

*Restored view of an early atrium house*

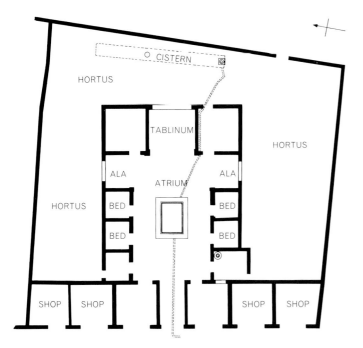

*House of Sallust, second century* B.C.

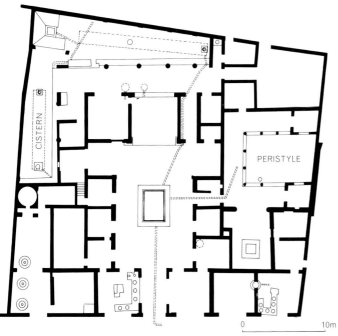

*House of Sallust,* A.D. 79

*Atrium in the House of the Silver Wedding*

53

arrangement of three couches (*klinai*) that constituted the normal dining pattern in classical times, and like the *cubicula* often identifiable from the layout of the floor patterns. Within the atrium one would have looked for such features as the family strongbox and the household shrine (*lararium*). Furnishing was by modern standards scanty, but it might include wooden couches and cupboards and small tables of wood or later of marble, as well as wooden doorways and screens. After dark the rooms were lit by means of oil lamps, often on tall bronze stands, and they were heated by braziers of bronze, iron, and terracotta.

This was the basic pattern of the atrium house, and with the passage of time it was developed and elaborated in a number of ways. The precise forms and layouts of such development obviously depended upon the particular circumstances of each house in relation to its neighbors, but once again the process can conveniently be summarized in terms of what was clearly felt to be a normal type.

The most important single innovation was a direct result of the ever-increasing exposure of Campania to the sophisticated civilizations of the Hellenistic world, where the standard type of wealthy house was one built around a rectangular, cloister-like, colonnaded courtyard known as the peristyle. These Hellenistic contacts made themselves felt at every level, notably in the character and wealth of the architectural detail and in the transformation of the old cavernous atrium by the incorporation of columnar supports for the central opening, at first four columns and later whole colonnades, until in extreme cases it came to resemble a miniature peristyle. But the most dramatic and far-reaching innovation was unquestionably the conversion of the old garden area beyond the house into a formal peristyle complex, accessible from the atrium by a corridor or corridors leading past the *tablinum,* which itself tended also to be opened up toward the peristyle.

For much of the year the rooms around the peristyle offered far more agreeable living conditions than the small, rather cramped rooms around the atrium, and there was an inevitable tendency for the main living rooms to migrate outward. One recurrent form, known as an *oecus* (a Greek name, which suggests that it was introduced in the same context as the peristyle itself), was an elaborately decorated room open toward the portico and often used as a fair-weather dining room. Another common innovation was the introduction of a private bath suite; yet another, wherever the slope of the ground involved a measure of terracing, was the introduction of a crypto-portico, a long, narrow, vaulted chamber or chambers, lit obliquely from above and useful for storage, or even as a hot-weather residential amenity. Above ground the open area of the peristyle was regularly equipped with fountains and pools, and with formal gardens in which plants and trees alternated with statuary and garden furniture.

The atrium-peristyle house needed plenty of space, and in the second century B.C. most of the wealthy householders could still achieve this by building out over their existing gardens. But in parts of the town one can already detect signs of what was to be a growing problem, that of increased population pressures and rising property values. Galleries and upper stories began to be added along the façade and around the atrium and, as street frontages became more valuable, more and more of the service rooms on either side of the main entrance were converted into independent single-room shops (*tabernae*) opening directly off the street, just as has happened to the frontages of so many of the palaces of post-medieval Italy, and for identical reasons.

54

*Peristyle garden in the House of the Gilded Amorini (VI, 16, 7)*

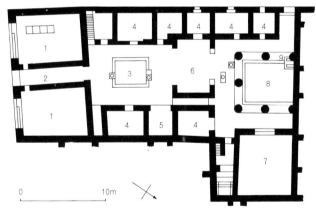

*House of the Tragic Poet (VI, 8, 3),*
*an early peristyle plan*

1. *Shops*
2. Fauces
3. *Atrium*
4. *Bedrooms*
5. Ala
6. Tablinum
7. Oecus
8. *Peristyle garden*
9. Lararium

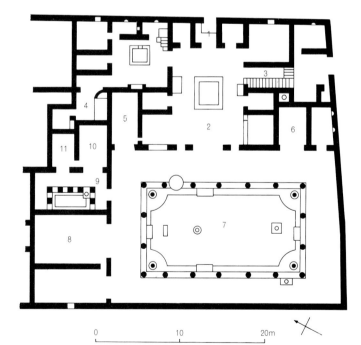

*House of the Vettii, (VI, 15, 1),*
*a late peristyle plan*

1. *Vestibule*
2. *Atrium*
3. *Staircase to upper story*
4. *Kitchen*
5. *Dining room (triclinium)*

6. *Dining room (triclinium,*
    *"Pentheus room")*
7. *Peristyle garden*
8. *Oecus*
9. *Small peristyle*
10. *Dining room/sitting room*
11. *Bedroom*

A third and more insidious change was inspired by the villas of the contemporary countryside. One of the more attractive aspects of Roman culture was its appreciation of natural beauty and of landscape. The town houses perforce looked inward toward their gardens, but by the second century B.C. it was already customary among well-to-do Romans also to maintain a country house (*villa*) — or indeed several of them. Although these were normally working farms (*villae rusticae*), many of them were also equipped to serve as occasional residences, and we regularly find these villas situated and designed so as to take full advantage of their setting, with terraces and garden rooms facing outward over the adjoining landscape. Within the towns scope for such development was obviously limited, but both at Pompeii and at Herculaneum we do find in the later period a number of fine houses terraced out over the walls so as to take full advantage of the views over the Bay of Naples, and during the first century B.C. the seaward façade of the Villa of the Mysteries was remodeled in the same sense. In practical terms, this opening up of the house was greatly facilitated by the widespread introduction of window glass, and although its full effects would not be felt in urban architecture until after A.D. 79, it was already a factor in the later planning of Pompeii.

*Seaside villa landscape, in the House of Marcus Lucretius Fronto*

The villas on the slopes of Vesuvius, at Boscoreale, for example, and at Boscotrecase, were of the sort described, centers of working estates that were also residences. But there were also the *villae marittimae*, the luxurious seaside residences that studded the coastline of the Bay of Naples ever since, in the first century B.C., Campania had become the preferred playground of the wealthy Roman. Inevitably their proximity affected standards of luxury and taste in the neighboring towns. Moreover, they were picked up by the painters of the Third Style wall paintings and used as one of the stock subjects for the smaller secondary panels of their large wall compositions. The seaside villa landscapes that one sees on the walls of a house such as that of Marcus Lucretius Fronto (see illustration) were *genre* pieces, but it was a *genre* rooted in actuality. Waterside villa platforms, jetties, harbors, single-storied or two-storied colonnaded façades with projecting wings or outcurving *belvedere* rooms, towers and balconies, temples and rustic shrines, grottoes, fountains, and statues: these were the commonplaces of a landscaped architecture as rich in contrived fantasy as any eighteenth-century English park. One of the sources of such paintings was undoubtedly a real, three-dimensional, luxury architecture, which itself owed much to what was obviously a very widely felt contemporary taste for romantic landscape — a taste that turns up again in the so-called sacro-idyllic landscapes and again in the conventions of the popular Egyptianizing "Nilotic" idiom. In painting we meet it already in the mythological landscapes of the late Second and early Third Styles of painting — the same trees and rocky outcrops, the same grottoes, the same towers, the same rustic shrines. Whatever the ultimate source of the individual motifs, these were all very much part of a contemporary Roman artistic fashion that affected architecture and painting alike.

Finally, a word about the gardens. In origin no doubt these were simply those parts of the individual building plots that were left over after the building of the houses, and were planted with fruit and vegetables for domestic consumption. In A.D. 79 there were still, behind the built-up street frontages, surprisingly large areas of open green, notably within the southeastern perimeter of the city, on either side of the Amphitheater and the Palaestra (which had no doubt been sited here because of the available open space). Here, as recent excavation behind the House of the Ship Europa (1, 15, 1) has shown, there were large

*The upper garden terrace in the House of "Loreius Tiburtinus"; at the far end is the open-air dining room.*

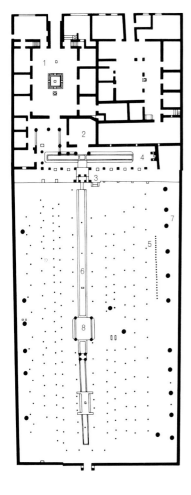

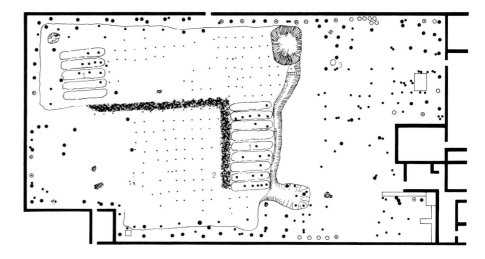

*Plan of the House of "Loreius Tiburtinus"*

1. Atrium
2. Oecus
3. Peristyle garden terrace
4. Open air dining area
5. Line of plants in pots
6. Ornamental water channel
7. Large trees
8. Small pavilion

0      10      20m

*Market garden in the House of the Ship "Europa" (1, 15, 1). Small dots indicate grapevine roots; black circles indicate roots of various sizes; empty circles indicate plants in pots.*

1. Vegetable gardens
2. Path
3. Water cistern

0          10m

stretches of market garden, in which vegetables were combined (as they still are in Campania today) with orderly rows of fruit trees and areas for bedding out young plants; there was also at least one sizable vineyard, in the block immediately north of the Amphitheater.

With time, however, and in the more densely populated quarters, there was an inevitable tendency for the garden to be absorbed within the architectural complex of the house itself. At one extreme were small, tree-planted courtyards, areas of shaded green upon which the occupants of the *tablinum* and the *triclinium* could look out: this was the logical development of the old Italic *hortus*. And at the other extreme, from the second century B.C. onward and, it seems, like the peristyle itself a newcomer from the Hellenistic East, we have the sort of highly organized, formal garden that one finds in the peristyle courtyards of such buildings as the House of the Vettii and the House of the Gilded Amorini.

It has long been known that these gardens were lavishly planted with trees and shrubs, and recent work is beginning to tell us a great deal not only about the layouts but also about the actual plants used. Not surprisingly, these included a great many of those still familiar in Campania today: olives, lemons, soft fruits, pomegranates, walnuts and filberts, chestnuts, and vines grown on trellises. Vegetables leave fewer traces that are readily identifiable, but here we have the evidence of wall painting and, most recently, a beginning of the results of the analysis of pollen remains. Paintings such as the garden room at Prima Porta (page 96) show that there were also cultivated garden flowers, but not, it seems, on any very substantial scale.

Perhaps the most surprising result of recent work is to show how large many of the trees were. Modern replanting has tended to follow the model of the later "Italian" garden, with low trimmed hedges and shrubs; and in the formal peristyle gardens, where the plants were a setting for fountains and statuary, something of the sort might indeed seem reasonable. But many of the smaller, courtyard gardens evidently followed simpler, more luxuriant patterns, including substantial trees. This has been demonstrated in the recently excavated House of Julius Polybius (IX, 13, 1-3), and also at Oplontis.

Within the town there was little room for landscaping: that had to be left to the villas of the seaside and the suburbs. But we do get a glimpse of it in the garden of the House of "Loreius Tiburtinus" (II, 1, 2), which sloped downhill from the Via dell'Abbondanza toward the open ground within the southern walls. Here the whole rear frontage of the house opened onto a transverse terrace, with a marble-lined water channel and a trellised pergola. At the east end of this terrace there was an open-air dining room, while a fountain in the middle dropped its water into a second, architecturally embellished water channel that ran down the length of the garden. Terrace and fountain basins were adorned with statuary, while serried lines of trees carried the eye down the garden toward the view across the Sarno plain and the mountains of the Sorrento peninsula beyond—a fine example of a studied formal design used to emphasize the beauties of natural landscape.

# THE ECONOMY: AGRICULTURE AND INDUSTRY

*Terracotta plaque set into a wall north of the Forum, showing two men carrying an amphora strung from a pole*

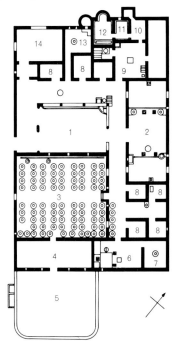

*Plan of a villa rustica at Boscoreale*

1. *Courtyard*
2. *Wine presses*
3. *Wine vats*
4. *Barn*
5. *Threshing floor*
6. *Oil press*
7. *Olive crushing room*
8. *Bedrooms*
9. *Kitchen*
10-12. *Baths*
13. *Bakery*
14. *Dining room*

The economy of Pompeii was based primarily on two factors: the boundless fertility of the Campanian soil and the town's position as the harbor for the whole area south and east of Vesuvius. Although industry was mainly geared to local needs, the proximity of large numbers of wealthy seaside villas must at the same time have furnished a steady market for surplus produce, for everyday tools and equipment, and for building materials. In addition to these local possibilities, Campanian prominence in the markets of the eastern Mediterranean offered rich outlets for spare capital, as well as numerous fringe opportunities for the smaller operators in which this region has always abounded and still abounds.

Fruits and vegetables of almost all sorts familiar in the area today (except, of course, for such post-Roman intruders as the potato and the tomato) are attested in the wall paintings and in many cases by the organic remains recovered during the recent excavations. In these, as in grain and other market produce, the city would have been self-sufficient. But the two outstanding agricultural products were undoubtedly wine and olive oil. Both of these, particularly the former, were widely exported, and they must between them have furnished a high percentage of the wealth of the rich landed families. Large numbers of wine amphoras have been found in southern France bearing the name of two of the prominent indigenous families, the Lassii and the Eumachii. Another of the leading local families, the Holconii, gave its name to a special quality of vine, while another prized vine was known simply as the Pompeian Vine (*vitis pompeiana*). The best known local wines came from the Sorrento peninsula and from Vesuvius; those of Pompeii itself were said to leave a hangover. The only surviving ancient picture of Vesuvius, from the household shrine of the House of the Centenary (see illustration), does portray the god of wine, Dionysus, decked with grapes, and beyond him the lower slopes of the mountain covered with trellised vines; the remains of the villas recovered on these slopes, like those of Boscoreale and Boscotrecase (see plan), show that they were not only the occasional residences of their rich owners but also the centers of working estates, equipped with all facilities for pressing wine and oil. Even within the city, excavation has recently revealed small vineyards, and the huge oil-storage jars are everywhere a familiar feature.

The one major exception to this predominantly agricultural, or agriculture-oriented, economy was the production of woolen goods. The wool was produced in the highlands of Samnium and Lucania, where some of the indigenous families still had ties and where many wealthy Romans had acquired large absentee estates. The family of M. Numistrius Fronto, for example, who was chief magistrate (*duovir*) in A.D. 2/3, evidently came from Numistro in northern Lucania (Muro Lucano, near Potenza) in the heart of the sheep-rearing country; and it was his widow, Eumachia, the heiress to a big local family, who built the large courtyard building near the southeast corner of the Forum to serve as the headquarters of the trade association (*collegium*) of the wool-traders and fullers. It was used among other things as a cloth market, and periodic auctions of raw wool were held in the forecourt, toward the Forum. The continuing importance of this woolen industry even after the earthquake of A.D. 62 is shown by the number of fulleries (*fullonicae*) that have been found in the city, some of them installed in what had previously been well-to-do private residences. The election posters, too, reveal the members of the association of fullers as active and influential supporters of the candidates for municipal office.

*Dionysus and Vesuvius*
*Naples Museum*

*Feltmakers at work (painted on the outside wall of a shop on the Via dell' Abbondanza)*

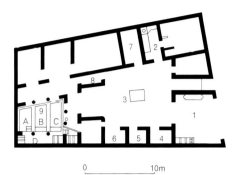

0           10m

*Plan of a fuller's workshop installed in a private house (VI, 14, 21–22)*

1. *Shop with treading vats and fuller's press*
2. *Kitchen*
3. *Atrium*
4–7. *Living quarters*
8. *Corridor full of fuller's earth*
9. *Peristyle with three large basins (A–C) for soaking the cloth, on three different levels, water draining from one to the next. D is a high walk at level of top of basins from which steps lead into the basins. E. Treading vats.*

The same election posters give us the names of a great many other trade associations, and these confirm the impression left by the excavated remains, namely that within Pompeii commerce was geared very largely to local needs. The associations named include agricultural laborers and smallholders, men engaged in various types of transport, dealers in poultry, fruit and vegetables, fishermen, bakers, goldsmiths. The list is not exhaustive—there is no mention, for example, of the important building and decorating trades—but it helps us to people the markets and the small one-room workshops in which, in the immemorial Mediterranean manner, many of them earned their livelihoods. A few local specialities went further afield. Cato, who farmed in northern Campania, advises sending to Pompeii for oil mills, or to Rufrius' yard at Nola. The building stone of the Sarno valley was shipped extensively to sites around the Bay of Naples, while the amphoras made in the local potteries traveled wherever their contents took them, including Spain, Gaul, and North Africa.

About industry it is less easy to generalize in terms that are readily comprehensible today. In the absence of mechanical power the factory even for a product with a world market, such as the red-gloss "terra sigillata" pottery of Arretium (Arezzo, in eastern Tuscany), was little more than a large group of related workshops, differing from those that supplied the local markets mainly in their number and organization. The only Campanian industry organized on this sort of scale about which we hear in the sources was the fine bronzework produced under the late Republic in and around Capua. It awaits detailed study, but it was evidently based on Greek experience and technical know-how, as already practiced in several well-known South Italian centers, notably Tarentum (Taranto), supported by ready access to the output of the Spanish mines, made available by Rome's defeat of Carthage in the Second Punic War. Already in the second century B.C. Cato advises going to Capua or Nola for bronze pails, water-jugs, and urns for oil or wine; and for a couple of centuries this area supplied much of the western Mediterranean, spreading its products up into central and northern Europe, often far beyond the Roman frontiers. At Pompeii itself considerable traces of bronze working have come to light outside the Vesuvius Gate; the Capuan factories and their Campanian subsidiaries must have been the source of a great deal of the fine bronzework in local circulation. Pottery was another flourishing local industry, both for domestic use and to supply the containers (*amphorae*) in which wine, oil, *garum*, and other local products could be stored and shipped.

Such in outline was the economy on which the manifest prosperity of late Republican and early Imperial Pompeii was based. But there are many signs that by the middle of the first century A.D. things were changing, and changing fast: the earthquake of A.D. 62 hastened, but was not itself the root cause of, what could well be termed a state of urban crisis. The prosperity of the recent past, based on Campania's privileged position in the markets of the Mediterranean world, was being rapidly eroded by the growing prosperity of many of the provinces. Spanish and North African oil were beginning to dominate the markets of the West. Gaul too was beginning to develop not only its own vineyards but also its own industries. Henceforth the bronzework of Capua found itself competing with workshops established in Gaul and, for the Danube market, in North Italy. A dramatic illustration of what this process of devolution could mean is provided by a crate of South Gaulish red-gloss pottery that was found at Pompeii, newly imported and not yet unpacked. Under Augustus the prototypes for such wares had been shipped from Italy all over the known world, from Britain to the Indian Ocean. But already under Tiberius an enterprising potter from Arezzo had set himself up in South France, nearer to his markets, and by A.D. 79 these South Gaulish wares were beginning to be shipped to Italy.

The results of this economic decline inevitably made themselves felt also in the social sphere. The established landed families were rapidly losing their virtual monopoly of local wealth and, with it, of local political office. During the last period of Pompeii we find their place increasingly taken by new men, many of them of quite recent servile origin. As we have seen (p. 44), awareness of some aspects of the process goes back at least to the beginning of the century; but while many of the new men no doubt retained their newly won family connections (it was common for patrons to invest capital in the enterprises of able freedmen), or indeed set about establishing themselves as landed proprietors, in the last phase of Pompeii there clearly was a considerable shift in both the distribution and the use of property. Some of the new men were very well-to-do: witness the reconstruction of the Temple of Isis after the earthquake at the expense of a man who had been born a slave. Nevertheless a surprising number of the old town houses were abandoned as residences and were being taken over piecemeal for commercial purposes. Of the private houses in the insula that contained the House of the Menander only one was actually being used as a private residence at the time of the eruption. The gentry were moving out. There was still vitality in the processes of municipal life, as the election posters show, but by A.D. 79 new social patterns were rapidly emerging.

*Painting of a baker's shop*
*Naples Museum*

*Bakery of Modestus* (VII, 1, 36)

# CULTS AND BELIEFS

Lararium *in the atrium*
*of the House of the Menander*

As might be expected in a society that was in a state of rapid transition, the religion of Pompeii during the last century and a half of its existence was a stream of many currents. The traditional state religion was one of practice rather than of religious experience. It satisfied certain enduring everyday needs both of the individual and of society; but in the absence of any consistent body of doctrine or of any fount of written authority comparable to the Bible, to the Koran, or to the works of Karl Marx, for example, it had little or nothing to offer those in search of higher truth. An old order was passing away, an order that was rooted in the needs of the family and of a simple agricultural community; and the new order that was to replace it, an order geared to the needs of the multinational society that came into being as a result of Alexander the Great's conquests, had still to take definitive shape. Everywhere we are confronted by a confusion of beliefs and practices. All that we can hope to do is to single out a few of the more consistent threads that went to make up the larger pattern.

One such thread was that of the popular beliefs and practices, many of them inherited from a remote past, which were, and were to remain, one of the enduring aspects of Mediterranean society. At one end of the scale there were the great gods of Olympus and their Italian counterparts, divinities whom the accidents of history and a powerful literary tradition had singled out for universal dominion; and at the other end there were the countless little local gods who so often lurk behind the well-known names. Great and small, together they represented the classical world's first attempt to come to terms with the forces of nature and the vagaries of human society. Like the local saints of Christian Italy (who were so often their lineal successors) they were the intermediaries to whom men turned when confronted by the hazards and seeming irrationalities of the world around them.

By comparison with this heritage from an older, simpler past the mystery religions were relatively recent. Classical Greece had had its Mysteries, but in the forms in which the Mystery religions made themselves most powerfully felt at Pompeii and elsewhere in contemporary Italy, they represent a fund of oriental religious experience to which the classical world fell heir as the result of Alexander the Great's conquest of the ancient East. More recent again, though derived ultimately from the same eastern sources, was the institution of the cult of the emperor as the symbol and formal embodiment of the well-being of the Roman state.

Few if any classical sites can equal Pompeii for the light they throw on religion at its popular, grass-roots level. The household shrines (*lararia*) that are such a prominent feature of the houses represent religion at its simplest and least articulate and yet, because it was obviously so much a part of everyday life, also at its most real. Traditional Roman religion was concerned with success, not sin: as Cicero remarks, "Jupiter" is called the Best and Greatest (*Optimus Maximus*) not because he makes us just or sober or wise, but because he makes us healthy, rich and prosperous." At every level of society religion was a matter of observance, not doctrine.

By Cicero's time the public face of religion was entirely in the hands of colleges of priests, prominent citizens who were elected or appointed to perform the proper ceremonials and rituals on behalf of the community they represented. Domestically the father of the family fulfilled the same office on behalf of the household under his care, offering daily prayers and gifts at the *lararium*, within which were displayed the figures of the traditional household gods, the *Lares* and the *Penates,* and of such other divinities as the family might hold in special

Terracotta wall plaques with a
phallus

Priapus painted on the vestibule
wall of the House of the Vettii

honor. Here too were performed the rituals associated with important family events, such as a boy's coming of age. These simple rituals were a part of daily life that no prudent Roman would have willingly neglected.

Yet another aspect of primitive religion that lived on into historic times was an emphasis on fruitfulness and reproduction, an idea closely associated in popular belief with that of good and evil fortune as active forces that had to be no less actively fostered or diverted. The Italian peasant who hangs a pair of horns at his roof tree, or who makes a gesture with his hand to ward off the evil eye, is acting out traditions that go right back to the patterns of belief natural to a primitive agricultural society, in which survival and fruitfulness are virtually synonymous. Many of the oldest Latin gods, such as Faunus, Silvanus, and Flora, had been concerned with aspects of agricultural or pastoral plenty; objects such as wreaths of fruit or horns of plenty (*cornucopiae*) were among the enduring commonplaces of religious symbolism; and the *phallus* (the extended male reproductive organ) is apt to turn up in (to modern eyes) the most disconcerting contexts: on a plaque at a street corner, on the statue of a minor rustic divinity, in the entrance lobby of a wealthy villa. The owner of the House of the Vettii, one of the wealthiest houses of the last period of the city's history, saw nothing incongruous in displaying in the entrance a figure of Priapus with a gigantic male organ being weighed in a pair of scales, as a symbol and safeguard of the prosperity of his house. Fruitfulness was an accepted and important fact of life.

Man's devotion to the little gods, even when they bore great names, is easy enough to understand. But what of the great Olympian gods—Zeus, Aphrodite, Apollo, Poseidon, and their fellows—whose quarrels and whose amatory exploits fill the pages of classical literature, and who figure so prominently on the walls of Pompeii? The Romans freely identified them with the gods of their own pantheon. But could any intelligent society take them seriously as divinities? Or were they little more than literary and artistic conventions, comparable to Milton's nymphs and shepherds or the Venuses of Botticelli and Correggio?

There is no simple, all-embracing answer. The old, anthropomorphic religion of the Greek Olympian gods was in truth long dead, killed finally by the collapse of the institutions that had given it life, and buried forever beneath the elaborate edifice of mythology that literature and art had built up around it. But despite the massive Hellenization of Roman educated society, and the consequent transference to many of the old Italian gods of the attributes and characteristics of their Greek counterparts, so far as the traditional religion of Italy was concerned these were superficial changes. Jupiter might be portrayed in the guise of Zeus, but it was as the time-honored guardian divinity of Rome, whose temple on the Capitol was at once the symbol and the enduring guarantee of Roman prosperity, that he continued to head the Roman pantheon. When in 80 B.C. a colony of Roman citizens was established at Pompeii, one of the first acts of the new regime was to convert the existing temple of Jupiter (Zeus) at the head of the Forum into a temple of Jupiter Optimus Maximus Capitolinus. This was not just a token of Roman political dominion: in terms of traditional Roman belief, it was the obvious and natural way of ensuring the continued welfare of Pompeii within the larger polity of Rome, of which Pompeii had now become a part.

[text continues on page 81]

Facing page:
**208**
**Statuette of Aphrodite with Priapus**
Fine white, translucent marble, possibly from Paros
Height 62 cm
Found on a table in the *tablinum* of House II, 4, 6

The group represents Aphrodite preparing to bathe (see No. 209), raising her left foot to remove her sandal and resting her left forearm on the head of a small figure of the god Priapus; a tiny Eros sits below her foot. Aphrodite's left hand, now missing, was carved in a separate piece of marble. The group is remarkable for the extensive remains of gilding as well as some traces of paint. In addition to her necklace, armbands, a bracelet, and gilded sandals, Aphrodite wears an exiguous, bikini-like harness. Her eyes are inlaid with cement and glass paste. The hair and pubic hair of both main figures were once gilded (the dark red paint now visible was the underlay), and there are traces of red paint on the lips of the goddess and on the tree stump that supports the group; of green on Priapus' pedestal; and of black on the base.

The statuette was found in the large complex of rented accommodation, including a bath-house and tavern, known as the villa of Julia Felix. *Graffiti* and other finds suggest that this part of the complex may have served as a brothel in the last years of the town's history.

**156**
**Dionysiac scene in marble intarsia**
Slate and colored marbles
Length 67 cm, height 23 cm
From the House of the Colored Capitals
(VII, 4, 31–51)

One of a pair of Dionysiac scenes found in the
*tablinum,* where they were probably used on the
walls as panel pictures *(pinakes).* On the left a
maenad dances in ecstasy, with torch and
*tympanon;* on the right a satyr clutches a *thyrsus*
and is waving a goat skin; and in the center is a
small shrine.

The technique is that of intarsia, a sophisticated
variant of *opus sectile,* composed of shaped and
inscribed pieces of colored marble *(giallo antico*
from Africa, *fior di persico* from Euboea, and
*paesina verde* and *palombino* from Italy) cut
out and fitted into a slate panel. Third quarter of
the first century A.D.

**247**
**Wall painting: entertainment after a meal**
Width 46 cm, height 44 cm
From House 1, 3, 18 at Pompeii

The central panel picture (now rather faded)
of a Third Style wall.

Facing page:
**192**
**Wall painting: Dionysiac cult objects**
Height 46 cm, width 46 cm
From Pompeii

Along a narrow ledge at the top of a small
flight of steps are, from left to right: a tam-
bourine; a wicker basket, on which are a drinking horn draped with a panther skin, a drinking
cup, and a *thyrsus;* and a second, taller drinking
cup decorated with vine leaves. On the steps are
a spray of bay, a pair of cymbals, and a small
panther grappling with a snake. All these objects
are associated with the cult of Dionysus.

**141**
**Wall painting: medallion with busts of
Dionysus and a Maenad**
Diameter 44.5 cm
From Herculaneum

Dionysus, god of wine and of ecstatic liberation,
is shown with a wreath of grapes and vine leaves;
in his right hand he holds a drinking cup
*(cantharus)* and in his left, resting against his
shoulder, the characteristic Dionysiac staff, or
*thyrsus*. Behind him, her hand on his shoulder,
is one of his attendant devotees, a maenad; she
wears a mantle and earrings, with flowers in
her hair.

**152**
**Wall painting: Phaedra and Hippolytus**
Width 1.03 m, height 1.04 m
From Herculaneum

Phaedra, wife of Theseus, King of Athens, had conceived a guilty passion for her stepson, Hippolytus, a passion that he rejected; where-upon Phaedra accused him of trying to seduce her. He was subsequently killed while out hunt-ing, and she hanged herself. In this painting Phaedra's old nurse tells Hippolytus of her mis-tress's love, as he is setting out for the hunt. The scene, of which there were several variant copies at Pompeii, is based on a Hellenistic original, which in turn was inspired by Euripides' tragedy *Hippolytus*.

**143**
**Wall painting: Pan and Hermaphroditus**
Width 1.25 m, height 74 cm
From the atrium of the House of the
Dioscuri (VI, 9, 6)

Part of the upper zone of a Fourth Style scheme,
from above the doorway leading from the *fauces*
into the atrium. Hermaphroditus, one of the
more curious by-products of Greek mythology,
was a minor divinity of bisexual form, with
female breasts and male genitals. In this picture
he is seated by a pool, and Pan, aroused by his
apparently female charms, has just discovered
his mistake. Beyond Pan is a tower within a
square enclosure, set in a rocky landscape. On
the right is a statue of Priapus, standing on a
pedestal and holding a cornucopia.

**299**
**Wall painting of a chariot race**
Height 57 cm, length 92 cm
Probably from the House of the Quadrigae
(VII, 2, 25), although the inventory books say
from Herculaneum

The picture, which is bordered below by a
red line but is certainly incomplete above and
to the left, shows four four-horsed racing
chariots *(quadrigae)* and, top left, the legs of
the horses of a fifth. The drivers *(aurigae)*
stand, as was customary, on a very light two-
wheeled frame, dressed in short tunics. For protection in the event of a crash (and these were
common) they wear tight-fitting leather helmets
and a harness of leather thongs on body and legs.
On the white ground below the picture there
are faint traces of an inscription painted in
large letters, which suggests that it comes from
a street-front, perhaps of a shop or tavern.

There was no provision for chariot-racing
at Pompeii itself, but many cities both in Italy
and in the provinces did possess a *circus* or
*hippodrome,* and as a spectator sport it rivaled
and eventually superseded gladiatorial contests.

It was organized into teams, or factions, the
support for which was Empire-wide. At first
there were only two factions, the Reds and the
Whites, but early in the first century A.D. two
more were added, the Greens and the Blues. In
the long run this proved to be too much for the
Romans, who at heart were as clearly two-
faction in racing as the Americans and the
British are two-party in politics, and by the end
of the second century A.D. the Blues had absorbed
the Reds, and the Greens the Whites, a situation
that greatly facilitated the expression of rival
enthusiasms. It was a clash between the Blues
and the Greens that in January 512 reduced the
center of Constantinople to ashes, leaving at
least thirty thousand dead behind it – an all-time
record for active spectator participation.

Following page:
**199**
**Wall painting from a household shrine**
**(lararium)**
Width 1.83 m, height 1.28 m
Found 6 June 1761 in VIII, insula 2 or 3

The painting is divided into two registers.
In the upper register, below three garlands, is a
scene of sacrifice. The *genius,* or presiding
divinity of the household, with head veiled and
bearing a cornucopia, symbolic of plenty, holds
out a dish *(patera)* over a marble altar. He is
attended by a small boy carrying a fillet (a wreath,
with ribbons for tying) and a platter; opposite
him a musician plays the double pipes, beating
time with a wooden clapper beneath his left foot,
while a slave brings forward a pig for sacrifice.
On either side stand the two Lares of the household, pouring wine from a drinking horn, or
*rhyton,* into a small wine bucket, or *situla*. In
the lower register two serpents approach the
offerings (of fruit?) upon an altar. Together with
the setting of rich vegetation, they symbolize the
fertility of nature and the bounty of the earth
beneath.

**241**
**Large painted panel with still life** (right half)
Height 74 cm, width 114 cm
From the *triclinium* on the west side of the
garden, which lies within the property *(praedia)*
of Julia Felix (II, 4, 3)

This still life, which is unusually large, comes
from the upper part of the Fourth Style walls of
a dining room.

A raised block carrying a large glass bowl full
of fruit (apples, pomegranates, grapes, figs). At
a lower level, a pottery vase containing dried
fruit (prunes?) and, leaning against it, a small
amphora-shaped jar, its lid tightly sealed by
means of cords attached to the handles.

**238**
**Fish mosaic**
Originally about 90 cm square
From House VIII, 2, 16

A studio piece made of very fine tesserae, laid
within a tray-like frame of terracotta, for use as
the central panel *(emblema)* of a larger, less delicate pavement, the design of which is not known.
It probably belonged initially to House VIII, 2, 14
and was reused when this was rebuilt in the early
Empire and incorporated in this much larger
House VIII, 2, 16.

Against a black background is displayed a
gallery of edible sea creatures, portrayed with
a lively naturalism that enables most of them to
be identified, in almost all cases, with species
still found and fished in the Bay of Naples. Among
the more familiar are octopus, squid, lobster,
prawn, eel, bass, red mullet, dogfish, ray, wrasse,
and a murex shell. The inclusion in the left mar-
gin of a small stretch of rocky landscape, which
is quite out of character, is perhaps to be ex-
plained as a fill-in taken from a different source.

**240**
**Four still life panels**
Width 154 cm, height 37 cm
From Herculaneum

Each of these panels was originally the center-piece of a large panel in a Fourth Style wall, as in the peristyle of the House of the Dioscuri. After being cut out, they were framed together to form a frieze. The first two are very different in style from the other two.
*a*. A plucked chicken or turkey, hung by its feet, and a rabbit hung by one forepaw.
*b*. Left, strung from a ring by its beak, a partridge. Right, a pomegranate and an apple.
*c*. Upper shelf, thrushes. Lower shelf, six pink mushrooms.
*d*. Upper shelf, two birds, probably partridges. Below, two eels.

**242**
**Three painted still life panels**
Width 129 cm, height 41 cm
From Herculaneum

Each of these panels was originally the center-piece of a large panel in a Fourth Style wall (cf. No. 241). After being cut out they were framed together to form a frieze.
*a*. Young bird and a light-colored pottery jug, over the mouth of which is placed a glass beaker with rilled decoration of a type frequently found in Campania and possibly manufactured at Puteoli (Pozzuoli). On the shelf above are indistinct objects: leaves, material, or possibly sheets of tripe.
*b*. Silver vase, with a small bird perched on its tall handle; a trident; seafood and shellfish *(frutta di mare)*, including murex shells; and a large crayfish. On the shelf above, two cuttlefish.
*c*. A rabbit nibbling at a bunch of grapes and a dead partridge hanging from a ring. In the window, a large red apple.

**243**
**Composite picture made up of four separate**
**fragments taken from Fourth Style walls**
Width 49 cm, height 43 cm
The writing materials and the still life came
from Herculaneum, the other two from somewhere in the Vesuvius area.

*a*. A silver urn, probably from the upper zone
of a wall.
*b*. Left, two book-scrolls of papyrus, one half-
unrolled; the titles, on little tags, hang from the
wooden baton on which the papyrus is rolled.
Right, a diptych, or wooden two-leafed writing
tablet (as No. 17).
*c*. Landscape: a rustic shrine with figures.
*d*. Half of a still life panel, similar to Nos.
240–242: an apple, a pear, and a pomegranate.

**302**
**Terracotta statue of an actress**
Height 1.11 m
Found with No. 301

The mask, shown fastened on with a band
decorated with little flowers, is that proper to a
courtesan in tragedy. The figure, whose left hand
was already damaged in antiquity, was colored.
There are extensive remains of the white underlay and traces of brown paint on the hair and
of blue and red on the drapery.

Facing page:
**309**
**Wall painting: tragic mask of a youth**
Length 62 cm, height 62 cm

One of four theatrical masks from the House of
the Stags at Herculaneum, where they constituted the lower parts of four of the vertical members dividing the middle zone of the Fourth Style
scheme into panels. Each is shown placed at the
head of the steps leading up onto a stage, within
a frame of garlands with Dionysiac attributes.

[*text continued from page 64*]

Facing page:
305
**Mosaic panel: rehearsing for a Satyr Play**
Width 55 cm, height 54 cm
From the *tablinum* of the House of the Tragic
Poet (VI, 8, 5)

The rehearsal for a Greek Satyr Play, the characteristic postlude for a Greek dramatic trilogy. The action takes place in front of an Ionic portico hung with *oscilla* (see No. 69) and draped with wreaths and fillets, above which is an attic façade decorated with pilasters, four large golden vessels, and a pair of herm-like musicians. The bald and bearded figure wearing a Greek mantle (*himation*) and sandals is the chorus master, possibly the dramatist himself. He watches two actors wearing goatskin loincloths, who appear to be rehearsing dance steps to the notes of the double pipes played by a richly robed and garlanded musician (who would himself have appeared on the stage). On the right an attendant is helping another actor into a shaggy Silenus costume. Behind the seated figure, on a pedestal, is a male tragic mask, and at his feet a female tragic mask and a Silenus mask.

What had changed was not the substance of traditional Roman religion, but the outward symbols by which its meaning could be expressed, whether in art or in literature. When Augustus built a state temple in honor of his own chosen guardian divinity, Apollo, or of the divinity who personified the military might of Rome, Mars the Avenger, it was as natural to have the cult statue carved in terms of contemporary Hellenizing taste as it was for Donatello or Carpaccio to portray Saint George as a youthful knight in contemporary armor. We meet the same phenomenon all the way down the social scale. Trimalchio, the parvenu millionaire of Petronius' *Satyricon,* had himself portrayed on the walls of his house as protected and sustained by Mercury, the god of commerce; at Pompeii we have an actual illustration of just such a situation. On the two doorposts of a dyer's establishment in the Via dell'Abbondanza are shown, respectively, Mercury and Venus, of whom the latter was doubly appropriate, both as the patron of a business that dealt in feminine adornment and as the patron goddess of Pompeii. Mercury is shown in the traditional guise of the Greek Hermes, staff and money-bag in hand, stepping from his temple to bring his blessings to the house; Venus, on the other hand, appears in one of her more exotic manifestations, as Aphrodite-Isis, riding in triumph in a chariot drawn by four elephants and escorted by the personification of the city bearing horns of plenty. The familiar images of the old gods, and of some of the newer gods too, had become a conventional language in which anybody might express his own individual hopes and interests; and it was because of the very familiarity of those images that they were able to convey their meaning.

With the mystery religions we enter a very different world of ideas. Whereas traditional religion had been a matter of influencing the higher powers through a discreet mixture of propitiation, flattery, and ritual observance, the mystery religions all in varying degrees envisaged the possibility of man's entering into some more direct relationship with the sources of divine power, and thus of obtaining special favor in either this world or the next, or both. To achieve this state one underwent some form of initiation, at which a "mystery" was revealed, and through which one became a member of an inner communion, with all its privileges and its obligations.

In the classical world, as elsewhere, the basis for such a relationship had existed since long before the dawn of written history. In any agricultural society one of the earliest subjects of religious speculation was almost bound to be the cycle of the seasons and of the death and rebirth of the crops upon which man's whole existence depended: the notion of the seasonal death or rebirth of some divine embodiment of these events is one of the commonplaces of primitive religion everywhere. In Greece the central figure in this annual drama was Demeter, goddess of crops and in particular of corn, whose daughter Kore, or Persephone, was abducted by the god of the underworld, whence through the intervention of Zeus she was each year restored for a spell of life in this world. The center of the cult of Demeter was Eleusis in Attica, where each year at the appropriate seasons the story was enacted symbolically in the famous Mysteries. The archaeological evidence at Eleusis appears to indicate continuity since Mycenaean times; the story (and by clear implication the Mysteries themselves) had already taken near-definitive shape by the time it first appears in literature in the Homeric *Hymn to Demeter,* composed probably around 600 B.C.

At what stage and in what measure the notion developed that the individual initiate himself underwent some form of divine rebirth and an assurance of a blessed afterlife it is very hard to determine. To ourselves, the heirs to a Christian

*Temple of Jupiter Capitolinus at the northern end of the Forum*

*Aphrodite-Isis riding in an elephant quadriga*

*Isis-Fortuna from the cookshop* IX, 7, 21/22
*Naples Museum*

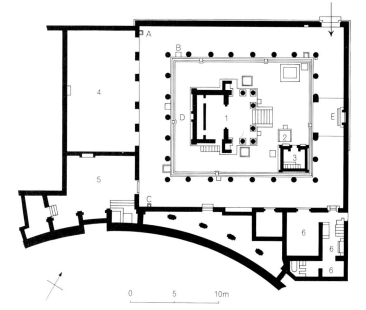

*Temple of Isis*    1. *Temple*
2. *Main altar*
3. *Building with water tank*
4. *Meeting hall*
5. *Initiation chamber*
6. *Priests' lodging*

A. *Statue of Venus*
B. *Statue of Isis (no. 191)*
C. *Herm of Norbanus Sorex*
D. *Statue of Dionysus*
E. *Shrine of Harpocrates*

culture within which the concept of individual redemption is central, it is not easy to envisage the attitudes of mind of a world where such a concept was alien; but the weight of evidence is that at Eleusis it was in fact quite a latecomer, probably introduced by assimilation with the ideas of the other mystery cults. The Eleusinian story plays only a very modest part in the funerary art of Rome, which is our richest single source for the strength and nature of such beliefs in later antiquity. Instead, we are confronted by the stories and the symbols of the mystery cults of Asia Minor, Syria, and Egypt: the Great Mother (Cybele) and Attis, Dionysus (in one of his several aspects), Sabazios, Aphrodite-Astarte and Adonis, Isis, Mithras, and a host of lesser divinities.

The content and moral tone of these religions varied greatly, and Christian apologists both in antiquity and since have been at pains to emphasize the differences between Christianity and the mystery religions. There were indeed substantial differences, but there were also a great many resemblances. Jesus' reply to his disciples when they asked him why he taught in parables: "Because it is given unto you to know the mysteries of the kingdom of Heaven, but to them it is not given" (Matthew XIII.II); or Saint Paul's, "Behold, I show you a mystery . . . the trumpet shall sound and the dead shall be raised incorruptible" (I Corinthians XV. 51) – these were words that would have been immediately intelligible to the followers of many other cults. Sacramental rites, including initiation and ritual meals; a theology based on the death and resurrection of a member of the divine family; belief in the readiness of divinity to intervene on behalf of those human individuals who were ready to accept divine authority, a belief often coupled with an emphasis on purity and morality rather than on the performance of ritual acts – in a great many respects Christianity and the mystery religions followed parallel paths.

The most obvious and significant difference was that Christianity, the child of Judaism, held itself rigidly apart from all other creeds, whereas most of the mystery religions happily gathered in all and sundry as manifestations of one and the same divine spirit. One of the most moving passages in classical literature is where Lucius, the hero of Apuleius' second-century A.D. romance, the *Metamorphosis,* calls in his trouble upon the Queen of Heaven (Isis), "whether thou art Ceres . . . or Venus . . . or Diana . . . or Proserpine . . . by whatever form of divinity, by whatever ritual, in whatever shape it is right to call upon thee." In her reply Isis acknowledges these and many other forms of her godhead, adding that "It is the Egyptians who call me by my true name, Isis." Here, out of the welter of ancient cults, we see the emergence of the concept of a single, ecumenical, all-embracing divinity. Christianity chose a simpler, more direct road to monotheism. But in the event, as it matured, even Christianity had to develop such doctrines as the Trinity, the special status of the Mother of God, and the communion of the saints. Old beliefs have their own ways of creeping back. As the heirs to a Christian culture, we ourselves have no difficulty in understanding the contemporary appeal of the mystery religions.

It was no doubt to her readiness to merge with the established forms of traditional religion that Isis owed something of her popularity at Pompeii. In the household shrines (*lararia*) it is exceptional for Isis and her co-divinities to usurp altogether the place of the traditional household gods, but they do very commonly occupy a place side by side with them. Isis in particular, in the guise of the Roman Fortuna, is found watching over every aspect of daily life. In a cookshop in Region IX (insula 7, 21/22) the owner, not content with the traditional *lararium* in front, had a second shrine painted on the wall leading to the

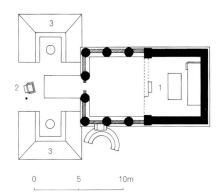

*Temple of Dionysus, at*
*S. Abbondio, near Pompeii*

1. *Temple*
2. *Altar*
3. *Ritual banqueting couches*

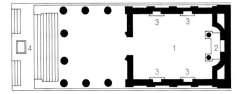

*Temple of Fortuna Augusta*

1. *Temple*
2. *Cult statue*
3. *Statue niches*
4. *Altar*

lavatory, in which we see the two serpents characteristic of such shrines, a gracious Isis-Fortuna, and the figure of a man relieving himself. At its most elementary, Roman popular religion could indeed be severely practical.

For a truer assessment of the significance of the mystery religions, we do of course have to look to their more organized manifestations, and here there can be no possible doubt that of the mystery religions current in Italy in the period before A.D. 79 the most popular and widely practiced was that of Isis and her consort Serapis (the Egyptian Osiris). Although the existing buildings of the Iseum at Pompeii all date from the period between A.D. 62 and 79, they followed closely the lines of a predecessor that was already established there before the foundation of the colony in 80 B.C. It took the form of an enclosed precinct, within which the temple, a rather exotic stuccoed and gaily painted version of a small classical temple, stood on a high platform, facing eastward down the axis of a peristyle courtyard toward a shrine in honor of the third member of the divine family, the child god Harpocrates (the Egyptian Horus). In the southeast corner of the courtyard there was a smaller building, with access to a subterranean vaulted chamber in which there was a tank, thought to have contained holy water from the Nile. Opening off the south portico, behind this building, there was a lodging for the resident priest, and at the far west end, behind the temple, two rooms that had evidently been added at some later date, at the expense of the Samnite-period *gymnasium*. The larger of these was elaborately decorated and served probably as a place of reunion and, very possibly, for the service of the ritual meals, which constituted an important part of the cult. The smaller, entered by a small separate door, seems to have been used at night (in it were found eighty-four small lamps), and it may well have been the scene of the dramatic initiation ceremonies that played an important part in this and other mystery cults.

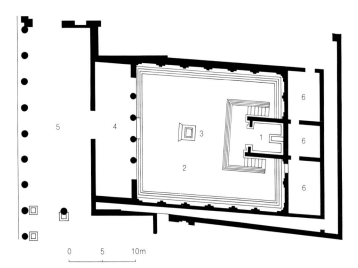

*Temple of Vespasian*

1. *Temple*
2. *Courtyard*
3. *Altar*
4. *Vestibule*
5. *Forum portico*
6. *Sacristies and storerooms*

*Altar carved with a scene of*
*sacrifice (no. 3 on plan)*

At the moment of excavation in 1764-1765 the walls of these buildings were still covered with paintings (the illustration is one of many sad reminders of how much was lost in that early work) and although the cult statues had been removed, the altars and most of the temple vessels and fittings were still in place. The central mysteries of Isiac spiritual experience are probably lost forever. But the Isiac religion was also one of elaborate ceremonial observance; here for once, in the temple at Pompeii, classical literature and the archaeological remains converge to give us a vivid glimpse of the daily rituals of one of the most powerful precursors and rivals of early Christianity.

Campania's mercantile connections and the large numbers of resident slaves and freedmen of Greek or Asiatic origin together made it fertile ground for the introduction of non-Italian religions, and there are in fact at Pompeii scattered traces of many such (for example, Cybele and Sabazius). But the only one to have taken a hold at all comparable to the cult of Isis was that of Dionysus (Bacchus) who, though long an adopted member of the classical Greek pantheon, was in origin a stranger from the lands to the north and east of the Aegean (Thrace and Phrygia) and one who had far too many disturbing overtones ever to be fully absorbed within it. Visitors to the "Thracian Gold" exhibition will recall the opulent drinking services of the Thracian devotees. But although Dionysus is best known as the god of the grape and of wine, he did in fact represent a very wide variety of religious experience, ranging from the uninhibited, ecstatic possession so vividly portrayed in Euripides' *Bacchae* to the sort of fine-drawn mystic experience to which so much later Roman art bears witness. His was a complex religious personality, and an aspect of it that bulks very large in art is its intimate association with the origins of Greek drama. It was in the Theater of Dionysus, on the slopes of the Acropolis at Athens, that the plays of Aeschylus, Sophocles, and Euripides were first performed, and the repertory of later classical art of all periods is filled with motifs that derive from this association.

In the absence of any substantial body of doctrinal or liturgical Dionysiac writing, the precise meaning of any particular archaeological manifestation can often only be a matter of informed guesswork, but it does seem that at Pompeii one would have encountered several distinct layers of Dionysiac belief and practice. One was that of domestic religion. In a town whose prosperity was so closely linked with the wine trade, it is hardly surprising that many individuals should, like the owner of the House of the Centenary (IX, 8, 3), have chosen to put themselves under the personal protection of the god of wine. Another aspect of Dionysiac worship, based presumably on the rituals inherited from Greece, was that practiced by the community of believers who established the small temple found and excavated outside the walls at S. Abbondio. At yet another level of sophistication were the rites and rituals of which the walls of the Villa of the Mysteries offer so tantalizing a glimpse. Here the worship of Dionysus was plainly a "mystery" based upon one of the primeval aspects of his personality, as a god of vegetation, of seasonal death and rebirth, and of reproduction. Common to all these layers of observance and belief was a symbolic language that was remarkably durable and pervasive. Grapes and vine scrolls, pine cones, ivy leaves, satyrs and maenads, panthers, theatrical masks, certain forms of drinking vessels: these are among the commonplaces of Pompeian art, so common indeed that they often seem to have been used as almost purely decorative motifs, with very little reference to their symbolic meaning.

What of Jews and Christians? Of Saint Paul, voyaging from Malta to Rome in A.D. 62, it is recorded that ". . . on the second day we came to Puteoli. There we found brethren, and were invited to stay with them seven days" (Acts 28.13-14). Members of this harbor-town Jewish community could well have had connections in Pompeii, and it is just possible that among them there might have been Christian sympathizers. But that is really as much as one can say. If there were, they have left (and indeed at this early date they could have left) no tangible trace that we can recognize. The romantically minded will do better to rest content with the pages of Bulwer Lytton.

The third strand in the religious life of Pompeii in its later years was that of the Imperial cult. The notion of the ruler as a divine being may seem strange to modern thinking, but it was one very widely held in antiquity, and it was one with which the Hellenistic monarchs had found it both prudent and profitable to come to terms. For a society within which the formal observances of state religion were a necessary condition of the welfare of the community, it was indeed a logical function of kingship to have a direct line to the sources of divine authority, and in the eastern provinces Roman rulers, from Caesar onward, accepted divine honors as a matter of course. Italy, with its long republican traditions, was not yet ripe for the overt, direct worship of the reigning emperor, but it was very ready to accept the sort of polite fictions of which Augustus was master. By getting divine honors conferred upon the dead Caesar, he became himself the son of, and successor to, a god; and within a generation cults in honor of his *genius*, his *numen*, and other similar personifications of his position as head of the Roman state were springing up all over Italy. At Pompeii the building shortly before 2 B.C. of an official temple in honor of the Divine Providence (*Fortuna*) of Augustus is typical, and there is an inscription (*CIL* X. 896) that records the building of a second shrine, dedicated in this case, it seems, to Augustus himself.

The establishment of these cults was clearly in the first instance a demonstration of loyalty, which might reasonably be expected to yield a dividend of Imperial favor; and it is significant in this respect that one of the very few new buildings put up in Pompeii in the difficult times following the earthquake of A.D. 62 was a small temple beside the Forum in honor of Vespasian and the new Flavian dynasty. But they also served another purpose. Whereas the major priesthoods were, in effect, elected magistracies and were held by such prominent citizens as Marcus Holconius Rufus (page 39) and his brother Celer, who were among the first priests (*sacerdotes*) of the Augustan cult, the day-to-day administration of the cult could be put in the hands of freedmen (and in one instance also of trusted slaves), at first as clients of the wealthy families, but before long as well-to-do citizens in their own right, thus providing a healthy outlet for the social ambitions of a new and rapidly growing class in the body politic—and a means of tapping their new-won wealth for the benefit of the community. The freedmen *Augustales* occupied a position of status and privilege second only to that of the municipal senate, the *ordo decurionum*. The *ministri Augusti* and the *ministri Fortunae Augustae* were smaller fry. Two of the three men named as *ministri Augusti* in a Pompeian inscription were still slaves. Their appointment throws a vivid light on Rome's extraordinary ability to attract and absorb the talents and loyalties of a potentially troublesome minority.

# ENTERTAINMENT, SPORT, AND LEISURE

*Hot room* (caldarium) *in the Forum Baths, Pompeii*

*Terracotta* telamons *flanking cupboard niches in the walls of the warm room* (tepidarium), *Forum Baths*

The public provision for exercise and entertainment at Pompeii faithfully reflects the city's mixed Greek and Italic heritage. At one end of the scale we have the public exercise grounds (*palaestrae*) that were the direct successors to the Greek *gymnasia,* that is to say places where a young man might pursue the physical excellence that was such an important part of his education. At the other extreme we have the Amphitheater, an arena for brutal spectator sports, which took formal architectural shape in Campania, but embodied far older Italic traditions to which Greece was a stranger; in between the two we have such buildings as the theaters and the bath buildings, which represent Greek traditions modified to suit Italic and Roman ways.

The old Samnite-period *palaestra,* beside the Theater, was in all but name a Greek *gymnasium*—a rectangular courtyard surrounded by elegant Doric porticoes, with a row of rooms opening off one short side. At some later date one end of it was annexed to allow for an extension of the Temple of Isis, but by this time its place had been taken by the vast new *palaestra,* undated but almost certainly an Augustan building, which lay immediately to the west of the Amphitheater. This was a huge rectangular open space, three acres in extent and enclosed on three sides by porticoes. It was shaded by orderly rows of large plane trees and in the center there was a swimming pool (*natatio*), the whole complex forming a magnificent public setting for such athletic sports as running, jumping, throwing the discus, wrestling, and swimming. There was a *palaestra* of comparable proportions at Herculaneum but, before the time of Nero, nothing of the sort in Rome. This was a specifically Campanian innovation.

Another, and in Roman terms more orthodox, development from the old Greek *gymnasium* was its incorporation within the newly evolving type of the Roman bath building—"Roman" because it was the Romans who completed its development and carried it with them to the remotest corners of the empire. But we now know that both the technology of the Roman bath building and the social habits of which it was an expression first took shape in Campania. The first public bath building in Rome was not built before 19 B.C., whereas there were already two in Samnite Pompeii a century earlier. Recent excavations

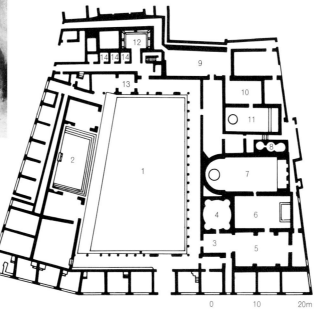

*Plan of the Stabian Baths*

1. Palaestra
2. *Swimming pool* (natatio)
3. *Entrance hall*
4. *Cold bath* (frigidarium; *formerly a hot sweating room,* laconicum)
5. *Undressing room* (apodyterium)
6. *Warm room* (tepidarium)
7. *Hot room* (caldarium)
8. *Furnaces*
9. *Women's* apodyterium
10. *Women's* tepidarium
11. *Women's* caldarium
12. *Latrine*
13. *Bath supervisor's office*
14. *Individual "hip bath" cubicles*

0      10      20m

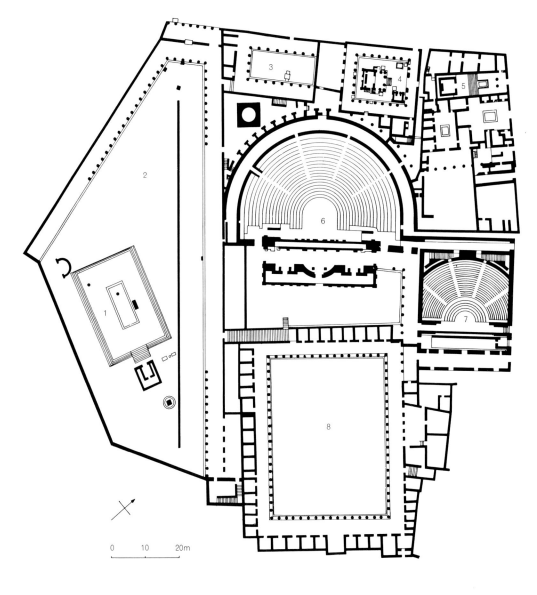

Theater complex

1. *Temple of Hercules (Doric Temple)*
2. *Triangular Forum*
3. *Samnite* palaestra
4. *Temple of Isis*
5. *Temple of Zeus Meilichios*
6. *Large theater*
7. *Covered theater (Odeum)*
8. *Gladiators' barracks*

0   10   20m

Small Theater

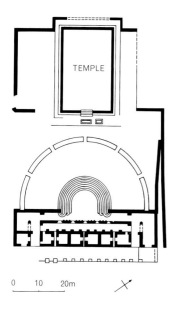

*Theater at Pietrabbondante*

within the Stabian Baths have documented in detail the gradual transformation of what had been a typical Greek establishment (as represented, for example, at Olympia), with small individual "hip bath" cubicles, into a fully fledged Roman bath, with chambers of varying temperatures heated by the passage of hot air beneath the floors and up through the flues in the walls, and equipped with hot-water and cold-water plunges—in effect what today we would call a Turkish bath, but with certain additional facilities. One of these was the addition of a *palaestra* for the taking of exercise before bathing. As the inscription that records the modernization of the Stabian Baths soon after 80 B.C. records, there was already a *palaestra* in the old Samnite Baths, and it was to remain an important part of the establishment down to A.D. 79.

The theaters of Pompeii (see plan) represent a comparable merging of Greek, Italic, and Roman traditions, once again with Campania playing a prominent part in shaping the merger. As regards both the forms of classical drama and the highly specialized buildings that grew up to house them, the classical theater was, of course, a purely Greek invention. It evolved steadily over the centuries; but it retained an extraordinarily durable hard core of continuity, as one sees very clearly, for example, in the visual conventions of the Roman theater, which were still steeped in Dionysiac symbolic imagery—an association that goes right back to the very origins of Greek drama, in the dances and sacred rituals connected with the cult of Dionysus. The original Samnite-period theater at Pompeii had been a Greek-style building terraced into the slopes overlooking the Stabian Gate. Later it was almost totally remodeled in the Roman manner, by building up the seating and by reshaping the relation of seating to stage and the form of the stage building itself; but one can still get a very good idea of what the earlier building would have looked like from the recently excavated second-century B.C. theater at Pietrabbondante (*Bovianum Vetus*), a sanctuary deep in the mountain country of western Samnium. This, it must be remembered, was a century or so earlier than the first permanent theater in Rome itself, the Theater of Pompey, built in 55 B.C. Beside the large open-air theater at Pompeii was later added a smaller, covered theater (*theatrum tectum*) or Odeum. This was built soon after 80 B.C. by the same pair of chief magistrates as built the Amphitheater. Except for the subsequent addition of marble paving in the *orchaestra* and the facing with marble of the front of the stage building (originally decorated with Second Style painting) the remains in this case are still those of the original building. It had an unsupported roof span of 20.6 meters, a good indication of the technical skills of the Campanian architects of the Sullan period.

What sort of performances would these theaters have staged?
For the more serious cultural occasions there was the Covered Theater, occasions such as concerts, lectures, readings of verse, or the displays of visiting rhetoricians in which antiquity took such a perverse pleasure. The Large Theater was, by contrast, a place of popular entertainment, and Rome was not the only society to discover that patronage based on popular taste does not make for a very high level of theater. It is not improbable that in its more serious moments the Large Theater may have staged the comedies of Plautus and Terence, perhaps even the tragedies of Pacuvius (who came from south Italy and bore an Oscan name) and Accius. But in the long run the Roman dramatists of the second century B.C. were to prove more important for the history of Latin literature than for the creation of a flourishing dramatic tradition. A single anecdote will serve to show what they were up against. Even in his own lifetime Terence, who died in 159 B.C., saw the first performance of one of his plays ruined by the rival

*Amphitheater*

*Marble relief from a tomb outside*
*the Stabian Gate*

attractions of a rope dancer and a boxer, and, at the second attempt, by rumors of a gladiatorial combat. By the first century B.C. tragedy had become an almost exclusively literary form, written for declamation or private performance; and although comedy was more robust (the texts of some of the plays of Plautus have survived because they were performed) it too was fast losing ground to simpler, more popular forms of entertainment.

It is difficult to present a coherent picture of this popular entertainment, for several reasons. One is that, being nonliterary or at best sub-literary, it has left all too few traces in the written record. Another is that at this level of performance the element of improvisation tended to be high and the demarcation lines correspondingly fluid. If we accept the distinctions made by classical writers, at least three well-known types of entertainment were certainly presented in the Theater at Pompeii: the Atellan Farce, the Mime, and the Pantomime.

The Atellan Farce would have found a ready audience. Named after Atella, near the modern Aversa, between Naples and Capua, it was a Campanian speciality, played in Oscan. Like the later Italian *Commedia dell' Arte,* or (to take a modern analogy) like many strip cartoons, it portrayed scenes of small-town life, revolving around the incongruous adventures and buffoonery of a few stock characters—Maccus the greedy clown, Pappus the gaffer, and a few others. Rendered in Latin, it had a brief semiliterary vogue in late Republican Rome, but it was really popular, grass-roots entertainment, bawdy, topical, and wholly lacking in sophistication.

Of all the forms of Roman theatrical entertainment, the Mime was at once the most elementary and the most enduring. Such formal shape as it assumed was derived from many sources, including no doubt the Atellan Farce and (another, slightly earlier Campanian specialty) the *phlyax* players of the fourth and third centuries B.C., who seem to have specialized in ribald burlesques of mythological subjects; but above all from the companies of strolling performers, the forebears of "I Pagliacci," who for centuries past had been dancing, singing, juggling, and playing their way from town to town, wherever they could drum up an audience. By Roman times, at any rate, they seemed to have abandoned the masks of Greek theatrical tradition, since the lead player, the *archimimus,* evidently relied heavily on facial expression. Like the Atellan Farce, the Mime had a brief literary vogue in late Republican Rome, but it was really, and it remained, a sub-literary form, deriving its vitality and lasting popularity precisely from its impromptu adaptability to the changing demands of local taste and of contemporary fashion.

The most sophisticated of the popular art forms was the Pantomime, which was introduced to Rome in 22 B.C. from the eastern Mediterranean, and which soon achieved enormous popularity. To modern ears the name calls up visions of the old-fashioned Christmas pantomime, but the classical pantomime was in fact something totally different, far more closely resembling modern ballet, involving the acting out of some traditional story in wordless gesture. The main difference was that almost the entire action was in the hands of a single player, the *pantomimus* (literally, "one who imitates all things"), supported by a chorus and musicians. A top-ranking *pantomimus* was the pop star of his day, the idol of the public, and often the intimate of emperors. A typical career was that of L. Aurelius Pylades, "the first *pantomimus* of his time," who had been born a slave and, after a successful acting career, was freed by the emperors Marcus Aurelius and Lucius Verus (A.D. 161-166). He retired to Puteoli, where, as a wealthy gentleman of leisure, he became a prominent local benefactor. At Pom-

*Phlyax players*

peii, as the *graffiti* make clear, the ratings of rival *pantomimi* were followed eagerly and the visit of a successful *pantomimus* was a major event.

The level of theatrical performance at Pompeii may not have been very exalted, but the Theater did undoubtedly play a lively part in local life. This is brought vividly home to us by a bronze bust, on a herm, which dates from about the turn of the first centuries B.C. and A.D. and which is now in the Naples Museum (inv. no. 4991; inscription *CIL* X. 1, 814). It was found in the Temple of Isis and it commemorates one Caius Norbanus Sorex, described as a player of second parts, a descendant (probably the grandson) of the well-known *archimimus* of the same name who had been a personal friend of the dictator Sulla. "To play second parts" was, in Roman terms, "to play second fiddle"; the Pompeian Norbanus Sorex was no David Garrick. Moreover, in the eyes of the law acting was one of the dishonorable professions, whose members were disqualified from holding public office. And yet here we have one of a pair of honorary herm-portraits (the shaft of the other was found in the Eumachia Building) set up in a popular public temple with the formal approval of the town council (*ex decurionum decreto*), by the *magistri* of the *pagus Augustus Felix suburbanus,* a body that one might loosely translate as the parish council of one of the country sub-districts outside the walls of Pompeii—not perhaps a very large pond, but in it a Norbanus Sorex could be quite a large fish and, by implication, a substantial public benefactor. Once again we are reminded that Pompeii was not Rome, and that, whatever the law might say, a successful local actor could be an honored member of the community.

The amphitheater was an Italian creation, in which Campania, with its hybrid Hellenized Italic culture, played a leading part. Rather surprisingly, Rome itself did not have a permanent arena until 29 B.C., and even then it was built of timber on masonry footings, not unlike the seating for the open-air opera in the Baths of Caracalla in present-day Rome. Before 29 B.C. displays of gladiators or of exotic beasts had had to take place under makeshift conditions in such open spaces as the Roman Forum or the Circus Maximus. This was a costly business, and it could be dangerous, as when the elephants displayed by Pompey in 55 B.C. took fright and stampeded. Keeping performers and mobs of excited spectators apart is no new problem in popular spectator sport. The problem was resolved, and it was resolved in Campania, by the creation of the *amphitheatrum* (literally "a place for viewing from all sides") consisting of an oval arena separated by a barrier from rising tiers of stone benches. The Amphitheater at Pompeii, built soon after the foundation of the colony in 80 B.C., lacks the grandeur and sophisticated planning of the later giants at Capua and Puteoli, or the Colosseum in Rome. But it has an honored place in architectural history. It is the earliest surviving example of an architectural form that is still in worldwide use today. It is also one of the first public buildings in Roman Italy to have used the arcade as a monumental feature in its own right. Campania at this time was way out in front as a center of lively architectural invention.

Although the Amphitheater could be used for any form of large spectacle, in practice what the crowd expected was blood, in the form either of gladiatorial combats or of performances involving the pitting of ferocious wild beasts against human victims or against each other. The provision of "games" (*ludi*) was a ready passport to popular favor, and one of the formal requirements of public office at Pompeii was the expenditure of a large sum either on public building or on public entertainment. The human performers were either condemned criminals exposed to some form of sophisticated butchery, or else trained gladia-

tors, who might be either the unwilling victims of circumstance (slaves, prisoners of war, lesser criminals) or else tough, voluntary professionals. They were organized into schools (*familiae*) under private or public ownership (in Rome itself they very soon passed into Imperial hands), one of the earliest and most famous of such schools being that at Capua from which Spartacus and seventy-seven other gladiators made their historic escape in 73 B.C. The possession of an amphitheater was a valuable civic asset, bringing in spectators from all the nearby towns. The disastrous Amphitheater riot of A.D. 59 was sparked off by the presence of large numbers of fans from Nuceria, a neighboring city that, in the best Italian tradition, was also Pompeii's deadly rival. It was natural that Pompeii, with its fine arena, should set up its own gladiatorial establishment. This was installed after the earthquake of A.D. 62 in what had been a large porticoed foyer behind the Theater (see plan, page 88). By A.D. 79 it was already partly occupied, and in it were found some of the fine armor and weapons now in the Naples Museum.

Every gladiator was a specialist, belonging to one of a number of conventional categories clearly distinguished by their armor and weapons and bearing conventional names. These names appear regularly in the literature and in the advertisements, and at any given time and place the fans would certainly have known exactly what to expect (and how to lay their bets) when a *myrmillo* from such-and-such a training school, with twenty-five wins to his credit, was matched against a less experienced but well spoken of *Thrax* from such another school. We today cannot follow all the nuances; when one recalls how even in as conservative a game as cricket the positioning of players in the field and the naming of those positions have changed quite substantially in the last fifty years, it is hardly surprising that the evidence from antiquity is not always consistent. Most of the main types seem to have been first established by the introduction of prisoners of war wearing their native armor and weapons, beginning with the "Samnites" in the third century B.C., and followed by the "Gauls" and "Thracians" and, possibly introduced by Julius Caesar from Britain, gladiators fighting from chariots (*essedarii*). Broadly speaking, they may be divided into the group of heavily armed fighters that evolved from the original "Samnites"; a somewhat more mobile, less heavily armed group of which the "Thracian" was typical; and a number of more specialized types, of which the most colorful was the *retiarus,* or net-thrower, who was very lightly armored (alone among gladiators he fought bare-headed) and who was armed only with a net, a fisherman's trident, and a dagger, relying entirely on his own greater speed and mobility. He was normally matched against a *myrmillo* (so named from the representation of a fish, the *morimylos,* which he wore on his helmet) or a *secutor* ("chaser").

The games followed an established ritual. After a public banquet the evening before, in which all the contestants participated, they started off with a procession (*pompa*), which was heralded by trumpets and horns, and which included the sponsor of the games and all the fighters, dressed in splendid costumes and wearing armor, which they would later change for their actual fighting equipment. After a series of rather tame preliminaries (mock fights, fights with wooden weapons, etc.) the serious business of the day began with a war trumpet (*tuba*) sounding for the first pair of gladiators, who proceeded to fight to the death, although there was a reasonable chance of a good loser being allowed to live to fight another day. About midday there was a slack period, filled with more mock fighting, assorted displays, and the executions of criminals, after

*A bar counter on the Via dell' Abbondanza*

0    5    10m

*Caupona of Euxinus* (1, 11, 10)
1. *Bar*
2. *Kitchen and latrine*
3. *Open air dining/drinking area*
4. *Vineyard*

which the afternoon would be devoted to *venationes,* in which wild animals were pitted against each other or against trained animal-fighters (*bestiarii*). Throughout the day there was a more or less continuous accompaniment from trumpets, horns, pipes, drums, water organs and, possibly, from voices. The whole performance is vividly portrayed in a marble triple frieze found outside the Stabian Gate (see illustration, p.90), probably from a large tomb: in the upper register, the procession; in the middle, on a larger scale as befits the major attraction, five scenes of gladiatorial combat; and below, incidents from the *venationes.*

To conclude this section about leisure activities, a few words about eating customs.

The Roman's single main meal of the day (*cena*) was taken in the evening after the afternoon bath. In polite society one dined on a couch reclining on one's left elbow. The average dining room took its name (*triclinium*) from the fact that it held three couches (*klinai*, or *lecti*), though a wealthy house might have several *triclinia* for different seasons, including one for *al fresco* dining in the garden; for a really large dinner party several might be used at once — carefully graded socially, if we are to believe the contemporary satirical writers. The couches faced inward upon three sides of a square, within which stood the tables and from which the food and drink were served. Three courses were customary, each consisting of several different servings, and wine (normally but not invariably mixed with water, and in some contexts served hot) was drunk both with and after the meal. The details varied greatly according to the taste of the host and the degree of formality. Frequently the meal was accompanied or followed by some form of entertainment such as music, dancing, acrobatics, or, if the host had literary pretensions, readings from poetry. Petronius' *Satyricon*, for all its element of parody, offers a brilliant picture of the sort of dinner that might have been served by a wealthy vulgarian in mid-first-century Pompeii.

For the man in the street and for visitors there were numerous bars and eating houses (*cauponae*), many of which also provided lodging, with or without female company. The Caupona of Euxinus will serve as an example. It was one of a number situated near the Amphitheater to cater for the crowds of visitors who came from all the neighboring towns whenever there was a show. On the façade was a painted inn-sign, with a figure of a Phoenix and two peacocks and the words *Phoenix felix et tu* ("You too will enjoy the Happy Phoenix"), and below it were two electoral posters painted up on the orders of the innkeeper, Euxinus, whose name and address are attested also by the inscriptions on three wine amphoras found in the bar: *Pompeiis ad amphitheatr(um) Euxino coponi* ("to Euxinus the innkeeper, near the amphitheater, Pompeii"). The premises were large: on the street corner a bar, with a typical L-shaped counter, a store, large jars for keeping food hot, and traces of a wooden rack for storing wine amphoras; behind the bar three other rooms, a storeroom, and a lavatory; and on it to the right a large open courtyard, which did double duty as a vineyard and, as in many a *trattoria* today, a place for open-air drinking and dining and, no doubt, gaming. At the far end of the garden was a painted *lararium* and stairs leading to some upper rooms; there was more accommodation in the adjoining house.

The *graffiti* found on the walls were characteristic, including representations of Dionysus and Priapus and tags of verse. One of these ran:

"Blondie bad me hate the dark ones. If I can I will. If I cannot, all unwilling I will love them still."

Tablinum *wall in the House of Sallust (First Style)*

Cubiculum *in the House of the Silver Wedding (Second Style* [IIA])

Cubiculum *in the Villa of the Mysteries (Later Second Style* [IIB])

Cubiculum *in the House of the Epigrams (from a drawing) (Late Second Style* [IIB])

*Garden Room, Villa of Livia*

Tablinum *wall in the House of M. Lucretius Fronto (Late Third Style)*

# PAINTING

The standard classification of Pompeian wall painting into four successive "Styles" was first enunciated by August Mau in 1882, and it still provides the best framework for any outline survey of the two hundred-odd years of painting presented on the walls of Pompeii itself and of the neighboring towns and country villas.

The First, or "Masonry," Style followed closely the conventions of the decoratively jointed stone masonry of which it was a gaily colored representation. Very similar work has been recorded from sites as far afield as Macedonia, Asia Minor, and Israel, and by the second century B.C. it was evidently already a commonplace of both public and domestic interior decoration throughout the Hellenistic world. At Pompeii it was already giving place to the Second Style when the interior of the Capitolium was decorated shortly after the foundation of the Roman colony in 80 B.C., and very soon after that it was generally replaced by the Second Style. The House of Sallust (see illustration) is one of the relatively few examples that survive in good condition. Relying as it did for its effect upon the patterns of the painted surfaces, which imitated in stucco the cornices and plinths, blocks and slabs of real ornamental masonry, it was essentially a style that emphasized the real solid qualities of the walls it adorned.

The Second, or "Architectural," Style began to come in soon after 80 B.C., reflecting the widening cultural perspectives created both by the foundation of the Roman colony and by Italy's ever-increasing involvement with the established centers of the arts in the eastern Mediterranean. The element common to all its very varied manifestations was a development of the wall surfaces in seeming depth, usually within a framework of simulated architecture; where the First Style had emphasized the tangible solidity of the wall, the Second Style did all it could to play down that solidity and to create an illusion of receding space. In its earlier stages (Style IIA), before the middle of the first century B.C., this took the form simply of making the main wall surface appear to be set back behind a framing order of painted Corinthian columns, which looked as if they stood upon a projecting plinth and supported a projecting cornice (see illustration). This was a direct two-dimensional imitation of a real architectural device already current in the earliest concrete-vaulted architecture of Campania and of Latium, and the resulting simulation of reality by every known trick of illusionistic perspective and lighting was to remain characteristic of the Second Style in all its manifestations.

At first the wall surfaces "behind" the framing architectural colonnade continued to be treated much as in the previous period. But quite soon (for example, in the secondary rooms of the Villa of the Mysteries, ca. 60–50 B.C.) this began to be accompanied by an opening-out of the upper part of the wall, as if the lower part were merely a screen over the top of which one could glimpse the open sky framed by receding architectural vistas. This search for visual escape from the sense of enclosure imposed by the inherited traditions of a compact, inward-facing urban architecture was to remain one of the dominant trends of Roman domestic architecture throughout the Pompeian period. The best known of all Pompeian paintings of this period, the Hall of the Dionysiac Mysteries in the Villa of the Mysteries, is in this respect an exception, Second Style in date but not in its composition. Not only does it omit the columns of the architectural framework but it also portrays the figures of the frieze itself as if they were acting out their parts in front of a neutral background rather than moving into and out of it. It is only in the small bedchambers (*cubicula*) that one finds the characteristic glimpses of open spaces beyond the wall (see illustration). In this respect the great figured frieze of this villa, like the Aldobrandini Wedding frieze in the Vatican Museums, is an intruder for which the precedents must be sought outside Italy in the Hellenistic world. Within less than a generation, however, this alien tradition had been captured and assimilated, and it is thus that we find it, displayed within a conventional Second Style architectural framework, on the walls of the Villa of Publius Fannius Synistor at Boscoreale on the slopes of Vesuvius. Despite its numerous and continued borrowings from, and links with, the larger Hellenistic world, the Second Style was evidently already an established Italian phenomenon, created for the houses and villas of wealthy Romans in the capital and in Campania, and faithfully reflected on the walls of the well-to-do citizens of Pompeii.

In the third quarter of the first century B.C. the Second Style (Style IIB) took a turn that was to affect the whole subsequent history of wall painting at Pompeii. The painted architectural framework, which had at first faithfully conformed to the simple rectangular shapes of the rooms it adorned, began to take on a life of its own, with each individual wall treated as a separate compositional unit, symmetrically balanced about the central bay within the larger symmetry of the rooms' three main walls. Both the painted architectural foreground and the wall surfaces it framed lent themselves admirably to such treatment. Among the many recurrent schemes one may note the development of the whole wall as an elaborately three-dimensional architectural façade articulated about three large doors, as in the Villa of P. Fannius Synistor at Boscoreale; the portrayal of a porticoed courtyard enclosing some central feature such as a circular *tempietto* (*tholos*) glimpsed between the columns and curtains of an ornately baroque columnar screen, as in the large painted *triclinium* at Oplontis; or, prominently displayed within the central bay, a large representation of a panel picture, usually depicting some mythological subject (see illustration).

Scholars have expended much erudition and ingenuity in tracing the sources of these compositions: in contemporary stage design, for example; in the fantasy architecture that graced the courts of the Hellenistic monarchs (and particularly that of the Ptolemies of Egypt); and in the elaborately contrived landscape architecture of the villas of Campania itself. That there was any single, all-embracing source is in fact doubtful; this was the expression of an aspect of late Hellenistic taste that no doubt found many outlets. But, making every allowance for an element of painterly exaggeration, it does seem clear that a great deal of what we see portrayed on the walls of Pompeii was rooted in real three-dimensional fantasy architecture. When, in one of the rare surviving passages of classical literature that indulges in contemporary art criticism, the architectural historian Vitruvius, writing about 25 B.C., roundly condemns this style for its "unreality," it is clear from the context that the reality with which he contrasted it was the sober functionalism of traditional classical architecture. Not for him the heady baroque fantasies favored by the avant-garde decorators of Rome and central Italy.

Two other famous surviving Second Style paintings must be mentioned because of their importance for what follows. One is the frieze illustrating scenes from Homer's *Odyssey* within the setting of a continuous landscape. Found on the Esquiline in Rome, it is now in the Vatican Museums. Scholars are divided as to the extent to which the "Odyssey Landscapes" reflect lost Hellenistic originals, but there can be no doubt about the degree to which this tradition of naturalistic landscape with figures had already taken root on Italian soil. In this case the landscape is shown as if glimpsed between the columns of a typical columnar order. In the Garden Room from the Villa of Livia, wife of Augustus, at Prima Porta just outside Rome (see illustration), even this formal restraint is lacking: the four walls simply flow outward, portraying in loving detail the trees and shrubs, the birds, and flowers of a formal garden laid out beyond a low fence. In this respect the Second Style could go no further.

If we have lingered over the Second Style, of which relatively few Pompeian examples were to survive another century of rebuilding and redecorating (and of which it is in consequence, very hard to convey any real impression from the few fragments available for exhibition), it is because this was the great creative period of Roman wall painting. This was when the basis of most of the subsequent repertory was established. It is common to speak of the Third and Fourth Styles as if they represented an orderly sequence of development. Development there certainly was, but much of it was achieved in terms of a repertory of inherited patterns and motifs, and it was punctuated by frequent references back to the recent past, the products of which were still there on the walls of the older houses for all to see.

The dominant characteristic of the Third Style was its renunciation of the search for an illusion of three-dimensional depth and its concentration instead upon the purely decorative possibilities inherent in the formal schemes it had inherited from the previous period. It retained the rigid horizontal symmetry of the later Second Style, with its two flanking panels leading the eye in toward the panel picture framed by the central *aedicula;* but although the formal vocabulary of the latter was still largely that of Second Style fantasy architecture, it was increasingly an architecture without substance, little more than a frame for the picture that had become the focus of the whole composition. At the same time there was a steadily increasing emphasis upon the fields of color and upon the patterns presented by the surrounding wall surfaces. Slender candelabra, trailing tendrils, arabesques of delicate foliage, abstract geometrical motifs— all these were used with an elaborate inner logic to create a formal unity covering the whole wall surface (see illustration). A good example of this can be seen in the Villa of the Mysteries, in the black *tablinum.*

Vertically too there was the same movement away from the illusion of real architecture characteristic of the Second Style toward two-dimensional schemes of balanced pattern. The plinth, the middle register of the wall, and what had been the zone opening out above this middle register, became three rigidly distinct horizontal bands of composition, linked by little more than the shared tripartite symmetry of the overall design. The gable of the central *aedicula* was flattened and compressed downward into the middle zone, to the upper and lower borders of which added emphasis was given by the introduction of secondary bands of small, elongated horizontal panels; the plinth became an independent strip of color set along the base of the wall and with its own independent ornament, while along the upper register were ranged groups of delicate, architectural fantasies, as far removed in spirit from the illusionistic Second Style fantasy architecture of which they were the offspring as the former had been from the "real" architecture with which Vitruvius so contemptuously contrasts them.

A third and very important component of the Third Style was its use of color to emphasize the formal divisions, and in particular the vertical divisions, of the design. A typical color scheme is that of the *oecus* of the House of the Menander, with its black dado, its green middle zone punctuated by black vertical members, and its white upper zone. To such wall schemes must be added the sober white

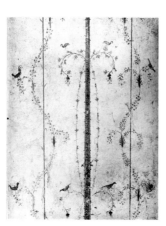

*House of the Red Walls* (VIII, 5, 37) *(Early Fourth Style)*

*House of the Centenary, detail of wall in the white dining room (Early Fourth Style)*

*House of "Loreius Tiburtinus"* (II, 2, 2–5)

*House of the Apollo* (VI, 7, 23)

*South* triclinium *in the House of the Vettii* (VI, 15, 1)

*Large landscapes on the garden wall of the House of the Small Fountain* (VI, 8, 23)

*Hercules in the Garden of the Hesperides (from the* triclinium *of the House of the Priest Amandus)*

or black and white of the mosaic or marble floors and the patterned polychrome tracery of the stucco vaulting. These were carefully studied, often sophisticated effects. To modern eyes much of the coloring may seem rather overpowering, but there was nothing indiscriminate about its application.

Insofar as it is possible to draw an arbitrary dividing line between two stages of a single, developing artistic phenomenon, the line between the Second and Third Styles appears to fall around 15 B.C., and the Third Style may reasonably be regarded as a direct reflection of the rather formal classicism that characterizes the official art that was just then taking shape at the court of Augustus. The earliest and finest Third Style paintings in Rome itself come from just such a milieu, a villa in Trastevere (near the present Villa Farnesina), which was probably the residence of M. Vipsanius Agrippa, the colleague and designated heir of Augustus, after his marriage in 19 B.C. to Augustus' daughter, Julia. If that is correct, the link with Pompeii is clear. The child of the marriage was Agrippa Postumus, born shortly after his father's death in 12 B.C.; it was in a villa belonging to this son found in 1902 at Boscotrecase on the slopes of Vesuvius, two miles from Pompeii, and reburied by the eruption of 1906, that a number of paintings were found, so close in style and content to those of the Villa Farnesina that they may well have been painted by one of the artists who had worked there (see illustration). This sort of thing, though we can rarely document it so precisely, must in fact have been common practice in the wealthy patrician villas of the Bay of Naples; when one sees how many such villas there were within a ten-mile radius of Pompeii (see page 16), it is easy to understand how, in style if not always in quality, the walls of this small provincial city came to reflect so faithfully and so rapidly the art of Rome itself.

The latest manifestations of the Third Style proper date from the middle of the first century A.D. (an unusually well-preserved example is the *tablinum* of the house of M. Lucretius Fronto ([V, 4, 9; see illustration]) and once again it was changes of taste at court that ushered in the fourth and last phase of Pompeian wall painting, in the years immediately preceding the earthquake of A.D. 62. This is conventionally known as the Fourth Style, but it might in fact better be described as a chronological phase embodying a number of concurrent stylistic trends, some of which reflect the extravagant innovations of taste introduced into the art of the capital by Nero, while others hark back to the recent past of Pompeii itself.

Space permits us to illustrate only a few of the more striking aspects of this Fourth Style. At one extreme we find rooms like those in the House of the Red Walls (VIII, 5, 37) and in the House of the Centenary (IX, 8, 6; see illustration), in which the walls are treated as a single sheet of color, upon which is overlaid a delicate patterned tracery; there is a marked tendency to reduce the size of the panel pictures, or even to omit them altogether. A favorite conceit within this *genre* is to balance a "White Room" against a "Black Room," as in the House of the Centenary and in the recently excavated House of Julius Polybius (IX, 13, 19—26). At the other extreme we find a reversion to the illusionistic architecture of the Second Style, this time, however, treated as a continuous architectural backdrop to the main action of the composition, which is portrayed as if taking place on a stage. Good examples of this are in the House of Pinarius Cerialis (III, 4, 4) and in the House of Apollo (VI, 7, 23). Between these two extremes lie a large number of rooms that are formally no more than an ultimate phase of the Third Style, more or less combined with elements derived from the Second Style or from other types of Fourth Style practice. A room such as the south *triclinium* of the House of the Vettii (see illustration) quite obviously incorporates elements derived from both the preceding styles.

Because this was the sort of painting current at the time of the city's destruction it bulks large in the surviving remains, yet its wider artistic significance is less. For one thing, the last years of Pompeii were a time of marked economic and social decline, a decline that was inevitably reflected in the levels of patronage and, in consequence, of artistic standards. For another, wall painting as an important art form was on the way out, to be replaced by marble paneling and, in really wealthy circles, wall mosaic. In this respect the eruption was nicely timed. Another few years, and there would have been little left of the older, finer Pompeii.

And what of the mythological panel pictures that were the most prominent features of so many Pompeian walls and that, torn from their context, have for so long dominated the modern image of the Roman painter's art? Very early on in the excavations it was realized that they were in some sense "Old Master Copies," based on well-known Greek originals, and for a very long time it was almost exclusively as evidence of these lost originals that they captured the imagination of scholars. It is only quite recently that they have begun to be studied in their own right as paintings that, though presented in terms of certain inherited conventions, are in many cases as Roman as the walls they adorned.

That they represent free variations upon the themes established by the originals, and not merely straight copies of them, is apparent the moment one compares the different versions of one of the more familiar myths. There are, for example, ten versions of the story of Theseus and the Minotaur derived from at least three different originals. The competence varies greatly, and those who wish to demonstrate the artistic superiority of the lost originals have no difficulty in finding telling examples; this was after all the work of house decorators doing their best to furnish their clients with a "Greek" art that was not their own, but that social convention demanded. But a more fruitful line of inquiry is that of the extent to which these panel pictures reflect developments in contemporary Roman painting. Here their real quality emerges; there can be little doubt that one of the most significant of such developments lay in the field of landscape painting, and in particular of the sort of landscape with figures of which Second Style "Odyssey Landscapes," referred to above, afford such an eloquent foretaste.

Although many of the standard motifs of Second Style landscape paintings and stuccoes—isolated trees, towers, rustic shrines, altars, columns, rocky outcrops—do seem to derive from a preexisting Hellenistic tradition of painting or stuccowork, few today would question that a painting such as the *Rescue of Andromeda* in the House of the Priest Amandus (1, 7, 7) represents a fresh and specifically Italian version of that tradition (see illustration). This painting occupies the center of the lefthand wall of a *triclinium* redecorated in a version of the Third Style that is variously attributed to the middle of the first century A.D. or to the years just before A.D. 79. Comparable figured landscapes, portraying respectively the Fall of Icarus and the story of Polyphemus and Galatea, occupy two of the other walls, while the fourth wall displays a painting of Hercules in the Garden of the Hesperides, which is a reasonably competent, if to modern eyes rather dull, copy of a Greek original (see illustration). The differences between this last picture and the other three leap to the eye. In it the figures are isolated against a neutral background very much in the manner of the figures of a carved classical relief; the orange tree, illustrated because it is an essential feature of the story, stands in the same plane, without the slightest attempt to convey

Rescue of Andromeda
*(from the* triclinium *of the House of the Priest Amandus)*

*Wild beasts on the garden wall of the House of the Epigrams* (v, 1, 18)

any illusion of an actual garden setting. This was the classical Greek tradition. The other three pictures are quite different in mood, composition, and treatment. It is the landscape that dominates, with its all-encompassing sense of real space, and the conventions used in its portrayal foreshadow to a startling degree those of later Roman narrative art. This is truly Roman painting. Ironically, but predictably, it was the "Greek" picture that got the post of honor. The educated Roman, hypnotized by the prevailing taste for Greek art, was notoriously blind to his own country's very real artistic achievements.

Much the same qualities emerge in the smaller decorative panels and other accessories that figure so largely on the walls of the Third and Fourth Styles. Still lifes, architectural landscapes, the Egyptianizing, or Nilotic, scenes that constitute the Roman equivalent of *chinoiserie*: painted in the broad, impressionistic technique of which Roman painters were the masters, they have an assurance and a directness that cannot fail to appeal to modern taste. This too was an art that had achieved a distinctively Roman personality.

One final question before we leave these mythological pictures. Was there any logic behind the choice of scenes? Did they carry a message, or were they simply the stereotypes of phil-Hellenic artistic fashion?

That many of the individual scenes carried widely accepted overtones of religious or philosophical interpretation there can be no doubt. Used in combination with each other and with the secondary motifs by which they were regularly surrounded (a great many of which had themselves entered the artistic repertory in the context of religious symbolism), they constituted a visual language that could be used to convey a remarkably clear and explicit message. Thus, the paintings from the villa of Publius Fannius Synistor at Boscoreale have been very plausibly interpreted as showing that the owner was an initiate into the mysteries of Aphrodite (Venus) and Adonis. In such a context the language of symbolism could be as subtle as it was eloquent, because it was addressed to people who understood what it was saying. At a more generalized level of communication, the mythological pictures are commonly used in what appear to be significant pairs, or trios, and some of these too may have been chosen because they illustrated the stories of the divinities to whose protection and good will the owner of the house aspired. Others (for example, the Trojan cycle in *Ala* 4 of the House of the Menander) may simply reflect the owner's literary or artistic tastes, although here too it would have been quite easy to read into them overtones of moral or philosophical meaning.

It does not, on the other hand, follow (as is sometimes claimed) that all of the mythological paintings at Pompeii carried a deliberate message. It is implicit in the language of symbolism that the more widely it is used, the more the precision of its meaning tends to get blunted. The terms become so familiar that they need a context to give them precise meaning, and in such a situation meaning tends increasingly to lie in the eye of the beholder. The workshops of Pompeii were not laboratories for the portrayal of belief. Under sophisticated patronage they could be so used, and at a more commonplace level any householder might select the current models that best suited his own personal tastes and convictions. But they remained essentially workshops, repositories of a body of established models, patterns, and skills; what they produced was determined by the fashions of contemporary taste, which to many citizens must have been largely a matter of keeping up with the Joneses. In the matter of giving more esoteric meanings to these paintings one has to take each case on its own merits.

We have dealt at some length with the formal painting that, by the very fact of its survival in such quantity, constitutes Pompeii's unique contribution to the history of classical art, and that, because it operated within a very precise range of conventions, does need some such explanation to be intelligible. By the same token we can be very brief in presenting the other facet of Pompeian painting, namely the popular art that adorns the gardens, domestic shrines, bars, and shopfronts. Simple, unsophisticated, direct, it tells its own story.

Much of this popular art was concerned with the portrayal of the well-known things of daily life: the shop of a baker (see page 62) or a potter, fuller or felt-makers at work (see page 61), a ship, scenes of tavern life, or of daily life in the Forum (see illustration, page 105). Occasionally it gives us a glimpse of larger contemporary events, as in the well-known scene of the Amphitheater riot of A.D. 59 (see illustration, page 34), but for the most part it was the work of simple craftsmen giving direct expression to what they saw around them. Even so, it was curiously selective: it was rarely used without some practical purpose.

It is at this level of meaning that one can most intelligibly draw a rational distinction between the spheres of formal and of popular Pompeian art. Although, as we have seen, the former could be used in sophisticated hands to express the religious, philosophical, or literary preferences of an individual patron, it was in itself no more than a repertory of motifs and styles of which the common denominator was the norms imposed by contemporary artistic taste. Popular art, on the other hand, like the popular religion of which it was so often an expression, tended to operate at a far simpler, more direct level of human experience. Nothing could be more stridently "popular" than the painted household shrines (*lararia*) with their great curling serpent figures and many of the street-front paintings were placed directly under the protection of the owner's patron divinity; advertisements of his activities, it may be, but also at the same time tangible insurances against the changes and chances of a capricious providence. This was a grass-roots art, shaped not only by its use of everyday themes but also by its expression of everyday attitudes of mind.

As in most such classifications, the distinctions between formal and popular Pompeian art tend to get a bit ragged at the edges. One sees this very clearly in many of the gardens. Here, side by side with formal Third and Fourth Style rooms are rooms and garden walls treated in a wide variety of other styles. Many of the subjects are borrowed from the small, secondary panels of the house itself—landscapes, scenes of hunting, animal landscapes, occasional mythological figures—but they tend to be treated in a far more relaxed manner, and often on a very much larger scale; typical examples are the huge landscapes in the House of the Small Fountain (VI, 8, 23-24; see illustration), the very large animal frieze on the garden wall of the House of M. Lucretius Fronto (IV, 2, 1), and the birth of Venus in the House of the Venus (11, 3, 31). Occasionally the influence was in the other direction, the garden influencing the house. Some miniature garden panels patently derive ultimately from such famous originals as the early Third Style garden room of the Villa of Livia at Prima Porta, while plants were freely copied on the dadoes of formal Fourth Style compositions, as, for example, in the House of the Silver Wedding (V, 2, *Mau* E). There was a marked tendency for the garden, its fountains, and its plants to invade the paintings of the adjoining walls. At the same time, the influence of wall mosaics was just beginning to make itself felt. The last phase of Pompeian art was one of transition toward a future that Pompeii itself was never to see. In it what had been "popular" art was rapidly acquiring a fresh, more monumental dimension.

# SCULPTURE

*Equestrian statues in
the Forum
Naples Museum*

The early history of Roman sculpture in Campania is largely shaped by the fact that by the first century B.C. there were few wealthy or influential Romans who did not possess luxurious country residences on the Bay of Naples. These were the people who, under the late Republic, were busy amassing private collections of sculpture inspired by the huge galleries of Greek loot on display in the temples and public buildings at Rome. Original works were naturally in short supply and contemporary Greek workshops in the old sculptural centers of the eastern Mediterranean were quick to take advantage of the growing demand for replicas and adaptations of old masterpieces. The letters of Cicero (who had two, if not three, properties in Campania, one near Pompeii) provide us with an entertaining picture of the lengths to which an educated Roman would go in order to furnish his country retreats with suitable statuary. The amazing array assembled by Lucius Calpurnius Piso Caesoninus, a rich but not exceptionally wealthy Roman, in his villa near Herculaneum (see page 110) vividly demonstrates the size and quality of one of these early collections. Most of the eighty-three pieces were acquired between 60 and 40 B.C., the products of various workshops. Among the many close copies and freer interpretations, which reveal Caesoninus' preference, in common with most of his contemporaries, for Archaic and Classical Greek originals, was a series of eighteen busts, herms and statues of Greek philosophers, orators and poets, and an impressive group of portraits of Hellenistic kings and generals. There were only two portraits of Romans, both of them historical personalities whose identities are in dispute, but no portraits of the family itself. Despite their relative prosperity the wealthy citizens of Pompeii could not compete on this level, but small-scale echoes are found in such bronzes as the Dancing Faun from the House of the Faun (Naples Museum, inv. 5002), the statue of Perseus from House V, 3, 10 (Naples Museum, inv. 126170), the statue of an ephebe adapted to a lamp-holder from a fourth-century B.C. original and found in the House of Cornelius Teges (1, 7, 10; Naples Museum, inv. 143753), to which may now be added a similar conceit from the House of Fabius Rufus.

It was not until the political stability that accompanied the reestablishment of central authority by Augustus that the erection of public municipal statues in honor of members of the Imperial family and of prominent local citizens became part of the everyday life of a small town like Pompeii. Once launched, the fashion caught on rapidly. But for the earthquake of 62 and the salvage operations that followed the eruption, a visitor to the Forum would have been confronted by a forest of statues. Three very large bronze statues, probably of members of the Imperial house, occupied most of the space at the southern end, and among the eighteen equestrian statues that stood on bases marshaled along the front of the western portico, in front of the Temple of Jupiter and elsewhere, must have been that recorded on the tombstone of the wealthy *garum* manufacturer and chief magistrate of Pompeii, Aulus Umbricius Scaurus (*CIL* X. 1024). Perhaps his is among those portrayed in a scene of the Forum from the Villa of Julia Felix (Naples Museum, inv. 9068; see illustration). About fifty other standing figures wearing the toga, the majority probably in marble, commemorated the services of other local worthies. In the surrounding public buildings and temples, here and elsewhere in the town, were numerous other opportunities to indulge this new craze. Among the few survivals are the herm portrait of Norbanus Sorex (Naples Museum, inv. 4991; see page 92) in the Temple of Isis (of which a duplicate stood in the Eumachia Building) and those of such conspicuous benefactors and donors of public buildings as Eumachia herself (Naples Museum,

*Bronze portrait busts*
*Naples Museum*

inv. 6232), Marcus Tullius (Naples Museum, inv. 6231), and Marcus Holconius Rufus (Naples Museum, inv. 6233), who were responsible for the fullers' hall, the Temple of Fortuna Augusta, and the rebuilding of the Large Theater, respectively.

It is at this period that portrait statues of family members begin to join the other sculptures in the Villa at Herculaneum, and portraits appear on semipublic display in private houses at Pompeii. Fine examples of these are the bronze busts of a man and a woman placed in an *ala* of the atrium in the House of the Citharist (Naples Museum, inv. 4992; see illustration) and the series of portraits on herm shafts found placed at the entrance to the *tablinum* in several of the larger houses. The most famous is that of the banker L. Caecilius Felix (better but mistakenly known as Caecilius Jucundus; see illustration, page 39), but there are also good-quality marble examples portraying successful businessmen who were well known in the town: Vesonius Primus from House VI, 14, 20 (Pompeii Antiquarium, inv. 407-4), Cornelius Rufus from VIII, 4, 15 (Pompeii Antiquarium, inv. 403-4), and the portrait of an old man (no. 26). Styles and techniques are so closely related to those found in public statuary that presumably, and not surprisingly, they were produced by the same workshops.

Such "display" portraits must be distinguished from the purely private aspects of family portraiture that already had a long history, among them stylized funerary statues executed by local craftsmen in local materials. The series begins about the time the Sullan colony was established and continues until the eruption. Another aspect is exemplified by the shrine of the *imagines maiorum* in the House of the Menander (see illustration). These are little more than puppet heads carved in the traditional materials of wood or wax, taken to represent the probably generalized and purely symbolic portraits that formed part of the ancestral cult. That this was still a living portrait form and not an extraordinary survival from a much earlier period is shown by the still unpublished wooden heads, on a larger scale, from Herculaneum, the best preserved of which appears to represent a woman of Augustan or later date. There was obviously an element of the population who, whatever it may have thought of the developing, strongly Hellenized style in vogue for public statuary, preferred to uphold, in a funerary context at least, the established conventions of an older tradition. Once again we see the "popular" forms and those more sophisticated trends influenced by the larger world existing happily side by side.

One of the saddest losses is that of all but a few fragments of the cult figures of the temples, among which must have been some of the earliest and finest pieces of sculpture that the town possessed. All the statues of divinities that have survived are secondary dedications within the temple precincts or from private houses, such as a Venus from a blue-painted shrine in the garden peristyle of House I, 2, 17 (Naples Museum, inv. 6412) and an Artemis (no. 4), all copyist works of varying quality and almost all produced in the early Empire.

With garden decoration we are again in the familiar world of Hellenistic imagery, and here one cannot help being struck by the extraordinary dominance of Dionysiac themes. These included all the rustic members of Dionysus' company and of course brought in all the characters of ancient theater. It looks as though there was a very strongly established convention in this field that the suppliers and their clients were content to follow. The only major exceptions appear to be the various animal figures allowed as appropriate to fountains.

There is nothing in the surviving works at any level to support the idea that Pompeii had its own school of sculpture. Undoubtedly a number of local jobbing workshops produced much of the simpler sculpted ornament on public fountains, wellheads, less extravagant tombs, and the odd figured group in local tufa like the naively conceived gladiator and Priapus commissioned by a tavern-keeper (Pompeii Antiquarium, inv. 11739). Some experienced craftsmen must have been charged with the daily maintenance and occasional repairs required by the growing quantities of municipal and official statuary. One or two work-shops specializing in funerary sculpture of the traditional type—a type found all over Campania—could have supplied the needs of the town in this context. But most of the major commissions, if not imported as finished works from Rome or Greece, would have been executed by the workshops based at Puteoli, where a steadily growing body of evidence attests the considerable activities of marble workers and sculptors.

*Marble head of a woman from*
*a statue*
*Naples Museum*

# THE OTHER ARTS

In a society that made no distinction between fine arts and craftsmanship, the "minor arts" were bound to play an important role. Although some of the pieces here exhibited were heirlooms or luxury pieces imported from other parts of the Roman world, the majority were made locally in Campania, which is known to have been an important center for the production of metalwork and glass, and which was almost certainly largely self-supporting in such things as jewelry, the engraving of seals and gems, stuccowork, and mosaic.

In the second and first centuries B.C. the long-established Campanian bronze industry, centered on Capua but with workshops probably in many of the neighboring towns, was exporting all over the Roman world, and although by the first century A.D. it was losing ground to new centers established in northern Italy, Gaul, and probably elsewhere in the provinces, in A.D. 79 it was still a flourishing industry. Its products await detailed study, but it is clear that they went in very large quantities to the European market, both in the provinces and beyond the frontiers. Although it was famed particularly for its large wine vessels (*situlae*) and other fine bronze tableware, it was certainly producing bronzework of many other kinds, including household furniture of all sorts, heating and lighting equipment, small-scale statuary, and statuettes. Several Pompeian families had connections with the Capuan industry, among them the Hordionii and the Nigidii, one of whom, M. Nigidius Vaccula, presented a large bronze brazier to the Stabian Baths and a bronze bench to the Forum Baths. Small workshops established in the town to undertake repairs may also have produced some of the simpler domestic utensils. Two *graffiti* mention coppersmiths (*fabri aerarii: CIL* IV, 3702 and 4256) and a bronze strainer found at Boscoreale is inscribed *pertudit Pompeis Felicio* ("pierced by Felicio at Pompeii"). In 1899 a partially excavated site outside the Vesuvius Gate produced quantities of scrap bronze, two plaster models of heads, a statuette of an ephebe brought in for repair, and a number of little bronze-workers' anvils. The coppersmith seen at work in one relief (no. 276) was evidently producing fresh work as well as undertaking repairs, and he was surely resident in Pompeii. Priscus the engraver (*caelator*) who greeted Campanus the gem-cutter in a *graffito* on the wall of the Palaestra *(Priscus caelator Campano gemmario fel[iciter]) (CIL* IV, Suppl. 8502) could have worked either in bronze or in silver.

The Roman passion for collecting silver plate was first fostered by the enormous wealth of treasure brought back by the victorious generals of the early second century B.C. from the Greek cities of southern Italy and from Greece itself and the East. At first it was available only to the very rich, who bought the booty sold at public auction, but silversmiths were soon established in Rome, producing plate in ever-increasing quantities, until by A.D. 79 we find even quite modest households possessing one or two pieces. Sets of eating silver (*argentum escarium*) and drinking silver (*argentum potorium*), together with one or two show pieces that were treasured as family heirlooms, were proudly displayed on special tables, such as that painted in loving detail on the precinct wall of the tomb of the young aedile C. Vestorius Priscus outside the Vesuvius Gate at Pompeii (see illustration).

Individual pieces from such services had been found in Pompeian houses ever since the excavation began, but a great many of the larger collections had doubtless been recovered after the eruption, and it was not until 1895 that a complete set of silver plate, 109 pieces in all, was found in a *villa rustica* at Boscoreale, two miles northwest of Pompeii. It had been deposited in a vat in the wine-press room (see plan, page 59), together with gold jewelry and over

*"Imagines maiorum,"*
*House of the Menander*

*Tombs outside the Nuceria Gate*

Mosaic emblema *of a Nilotic landscape (House of the Menander)*

*Display of silver plate painted on the wall of the tomb of Vestorius Priscus*

one thousand gold coins, and beside it lay the skeleton of a woman. The collection had been made very largely in the early years of the first century A.D., but it also included a dish over three hundred years old and there were some later purchases. As well as drinking cups and eating dishes there were also some display pieces and toilet mirrors.

In 1930 this hoard was matched by the discovery of a similar treasure in an underground room of the House of the Menander (see plan, page 48), where it had been stored for safekeeping in a large wooden chest, reinforced with bronze, each piece carefully wrapped in a cloth and neatly arranged in series. It comprised 118 pieces, weighing a total of just under 53 pounds (24 kilograms). Alongside it was found the family jewelry, which included a *bulla* and a number of gold and silver coins, carefully chosen (as is customary in such stores of reserve coinage) from issues that, because of their gold or silver content, were secure against the inflation that was already steadily eroding the value of ordinary contemporary coinage. Most of the vessels were probably produced by the workshops in Rome, but there were silversmiths from southern Italy and Greece resident in Neapolis and Puteoli who could as easily have supplied the more strongly Hellenistic forms. The carefully executed repairs made to some of the silverware found would certainly have been done locally.

Goldsmiths and gem-cutters were among the small craftsmen of Pompeii. The *aurifices* declared themselves as supporters of an electoral candidate, and Campanus, a *gemmarius*, is hailed by the metal-engraver (*caelator*) Priscus. A dealer or cutter of gemstones, Pinarius Cerialis, lived in a house (III, 4b) on the Via dell'Abbondanza, in which were found some engraving tools and a box containing 114 cut and partially worked carnelians, sardonyx, amethysts, and agates.

Most of the fine glass found in Pompeii probably came from Puteoli, where glassblowing was a major industry. No glass furnaces have yet been found at Pompeii itself, but these would in any case have tended to be located outside the residential districts in areas as yet only very summarily explored. There are, moreover, several rather simple forms—a particular type of plain beaker, for example, and a special form of squat, handled wine jug (*askos*)—that appear to be peculiar to Pompeii. It seems likely that, like jobbing bronze-workers, small potters, and lamp-makers, there were also glass-workers catering for the simple everyday needs of the town.

Among the other craftsmen active at Pompeii, there were a great many painters, mosaicists, and stuccoists. The almost total absence of any reference to them in the inscriptions and in the *graffiti* does, however, suggest that, as at many other periods of history, such men tended to travel wherever their skills were required, and that most of them were based elsewhere in Campania. There was also a measure of centralized workshop production for some of the finest pieces, such as the mosaic *emblemata* that constituted the highly prized centerpieces of many of the best pavements (as in the House of the Menander; see illustration) and that were made in specially transportable trays. The same would have applied to the painted *pinakes* that, being on wood, have almost all perished. In both cases one thinks naturally of Neapolis, that great local center of conservative Greek culture, the Roman-period archaeology of which is probably lost to us forever.

# HERCULANEUM

Herculaneum lay on the coast, on a spur projecting from the foot of Vesuvius, about five miles east of Neapolis (Naples) and ten miles west of Pompeii. The ancient coastline is today so overlaid by later deposits that it calls for a strong effort of the imagination to picture Herculaneum as it is described by the first-century-B.C. historian Sisenna, namely as a small city set on a headland between two inlets that served as harbors. Dionysius of Halicarnassus refers to the excellence of these harbors, and Strabo refers to it as an unusually healthy place. To judge from the few references in ancient literature (and archaeology has as yet barely touched the earlier levels) its early history was very similar to that of Pompeii. Founded probably as a fortified Greek trading post, it passed with Pompeii under Samnite rule. During the Social War it was occupied by Sulla's troops in 89 B.C., but there is no evidence to indicate that, like Pompeii, it was refounded as a Roman colony. Instead, at about this time it seems to have acquired the status of a municipality (*municipium*), a status that involved the establishment of municipal institutions closely akin to those of a *colonia*, but without any expropriations of property or the introduction of fresh citizens from outside. Though badly damaged in the earthquake of A.D. 62, Herculaneum made a more rapid recovery than Pompeii. Within the area excavated much is rebuilt or redecorated, but there is little unfinished work. In broad essentials the two cities continued to have much in common, enough certainly to justify the use of exhibits from Herculaneum wherever, for one reason or another, comparable material is not available from Pompeii.

There were, however, also significant differences, of which two in particular deserve mention here. One is that whereas Pompeii, thanks to its position at the mouth of the river Sarno, became a prosperous local port and market town, Herculaneum developed on more exclusively residential lines. Some local commerce it did of course have: the main coast road ran straight across the town, of which it was one of the principal transverse streets, and the harbor was the natural outlet for the vineyards of the southern slopes of Vesuvius. But one has only to walk through the streets of the excavated quarter to sense the difference of atmosphere: almost exclusively residential, with shops and bars grouped along two of the main streets and very little trace of local industry. Herculaneum's role was that of a miniature Brighton, profiting from its salubrious climate and from the proximity of many wealthy villas. One of these, the Villa of the Papyri, the property of L. Calpurnius Piso Caesoninus, the father-in-law of Caesar, lay just outside the west gate. Here, eighteenth-century tunneling brought to light a unique series of late Hellenistic bronze sculptures and a library of more than a thousand papyrus rolls, most of them—such are the ironies of archaeological survival—the works of minor Epicurean philosophers. The area of the city so far uncovered, running southward from the main cross-street toward the southeastern part of the sea frontage of the promontory, is laid out on a street grid of Greek type. Among the public buildings excavated, or explored by tunneled galleries in the eighteenth-century manner, are a small but richly adorned theater; a building opening off the main street that may or may not prove to have been a basilica; two public bath buildings, one within the town and akin to the Stabian baths and a more modern building outside the walls; and on the east side of the town a large *palaestra* similar to that near the Amphitheater at Pompeii. Still to be located, but known from inscriptions, are a market building (*macellum*), a temple of Isis, and a temple of Magna Mater, the predecessor of which had been destroyed by the earthquake and was restored in A.D. 76 through the bounty of the emperor Vespasian.

*Herculaneum*

A second and to ourselves very important distinction between Pompeii and Herculaneum is the very different manner in which they were hit by the final catastrophe, a circumstance that has materially affected the nature and condition of the surviving remains. Whereas Pompeii was slowly but inexorably engulfed by layer upon layer of airborne, sulphurous debris, at Herculaneum the destruction took place in two sharply distinguishable stages. The initial bombardment of incandescent pebbles and rocks resulting from the first explosion may well have been more intense than at Pompeii; it will be recalled (see page 37) that a few hours later Pliny the Elder was already unable to put ashore here and had to coast down to Stabiae. But there was not much ash, and most of the inhabitants seem to have been able to make good their escape up the road to Naples. Relatively few bodies have been found within the city. Then came the second stage, in which the town was engulfed by a horrendous avalanche of liquid mud, swept down the mountainside by the torrential rains that frequently accompany an eruption, and channeled toward Herculaneum by the valleys of which the city's two harbors were the mouths. A wall of mud flooded through the streets and into the houses, bringing down the roofs of some and filling up others. When the area became once more accessible, the coastline had changed beyond all recognition. The city lay buried beneath a mantle of deposit in places as much as sixty-five feet deep, which was rapidly hardening into the solid rock through which well-diggers in the early eighteenth century chanced upon the Roman theater, and upon which the houses of the modern Resina now stand.

This sequence of events had several important consequences. One is that whatever was not destroyed by the first impact of fire and mud was securely sealed against all intrusion until modern times. At Pompeii few of the public buildings or the wealthier houses escaped the post-eruption attentions of their owners or of looters. They could be located because many of the taller landmarks were still visible, and although it was dangerous work (and some of the bodies found are certainly those of looters rather than of eruption victims), there were rich prizes to be won. The Forum area was stripped of its bronze statuary and much of its marble and fine building stone, and private houses were ransacked for their treasure chests and other valuables. At Herculaneum all that was not removed during the first few hours of the eruption was preserved for posterity. Sadly, the eighteenth-century treasure hunters destroyed far more than they recovered, but even so we have a unique body of public statuary found as and where it was used in antiquity. Another consequence was the preservation not merely of the impressions of organic objects, but also in many cases of the actual carbonized remains of the objects themselves, such things as furnishings and woodwork, doors and screens, foodstuffs, or the papyrus rolls referred to above. Such objects are, alas, too fragile to travel, but they have added very materially to our knowledge of many aspects of daily life in antiquity, which in normal circumstances are irrevocably lost.